Best 100

Best 100

Favorite Recipes from
America's Most Trusted Cook

Houghton Mifflin Harcourt | Boston | New York | 2021

GENERAL MILLS

Vice President Digital,
Data & Analytics: David Bernard

Global Business Solutions Manager:
Christine Gray

Executive Editor: Cathy
Swanson Wheaton

Recipe Development and Testing:
Betty Crocker Kitchens

Photography: General Mills
Photography Studios and Tony
Kubat Photography

HOUGHTON MIFFLIN HARCOURT

Editorial Director: Karen Murgolo

Editor: Sarah Kwak

Senior Managing Editor:
Marina Padakis

Senior Editor: Christina Stambaugh

Art Director and Book Design:
Tai Blanche

Lead Production Coordinator:
Kimberly Kiefer

Published by Houghton Mifflin Harcourt Publishing Company

For information about permission to reproduce selections from this book, write to Permissions, Houghton Mifflin Harcourt Publishing Company, 3 Park Avenue, New York, New York 10016.

www.hmhbooks.com

Library of Congress Cataloging-in-Publication Data:

Names: Crocker, Betty, author. | Betty Crocker Kitchens.
Title: Betty Crocker best 100 : favorite recipes from America's most trusted cook / Betty Crocker.
Other titles: best 100
Description: Boston : Houghton Mifflin Harcourt, [2021] | Includes index.
Identifiers: LCCN 2021010014 (print) | LCCN 2021010015 (ebook) | ISBN 9780358381136 (hardback) | ISBN 9780358379690 (ebook)
Subjects: LCSH: Cooking. | BISAC: COOKING / Regional & Ethnic / American / General | COOKING / Courses & Dishes / Casseroles | LCGFT: Cookbooks.
Classification: LCC TX714 .C7514 2021 (print) | LCC TX714 (ebook) | DDC 641.5—dc23
LC record available at https://lccn.loc.gov/2021010014
LC ebook record available at https://lccn.loc.gov/2021010015

Manufactured in China

SCP 10 9 8 7 6 5 4 3 2 1

Find more great ideas at BettyCrocker.com

Dear Makers,

100 years is a big reason to celebrate. 100 years of history in the baking of literally thousands of kitchen-tested recipes that have been stirring things up for generations. It's always been about recognizing that the kitchen is the heart of the home and the joy of sharing good food is a magnet that connects us with those we love.

Makers get that when you cook, it has the power to stretch a food budget, beckon a sleepy head from their slumber, teach while sharing a fun, delicious experience and create memories. I've been the friend in kitchens everywhere, sharing what I know about cooking and anything related to food, sparking your own "cheffiness" to make dishes you're proud to serve, which in turn, ignites conversations and invites laughter at the countertop, the dinner table and the backyard patio.

Great, well-written recipes lead to amazing dishes, no matter what your cooking experience. This book gathers the best tried-and-true favorites that have risen to the top of the Betty Crocker Kitchens recipe card box. Whether transcending the decades or lovingly updated for today's trends and tastes, they're all incredibly delicious and sure to be a success because as always, they have been thoroughly tested in the most-trusted test kitchens in America, the Betty Crocker Kitchens.

Also sprinkled throughout this book is a look back at my story and how I've come to be (and still am) one of the most recognized names in America. 100 years later, I'm still stirring up recipes to trend with the times and sharing the wealth of my cooking knowledge; empowering you in the kitchen to create your own magical food connectors. So, put on your apron (your supercape).

Let's get making!

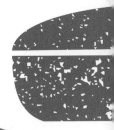

Contents

The Many Faces of Betty Crocker

Betty Crocker—100 years old and still one of the most recognized names in America! Betty was born in 1921, but not in a hospital or at the hand of a midwife. She was born in an office! Spoiler alert: Betty is NOT a real person. When the makers of Gold Medal™ flour held a contest asking people to solve a puzzle and send it in to receive a free flour sack pin cushion, what they got back was more than completed puzzles. Consumers also sent in questions by the hundreds, asking for help in cooking and baking. The executives at the company decided that there should be a personality created who would respond to consumers' questions and provide recipes as well as cooking and baking advice.

And so, Betty was born. Company executives took the name "Betty," a popular, friendly sounding name of the time, and paired it with "Crocker," the name of a beloved retired leader of the company. A paper was passed around the office, and everyone wrote her signature until one was found that they liked, and it became her signature "signature"!

1936

Betty's First Portrait

Never seen before her 15th birthday, Betty officially debuted in a formal portrait. Betty embodied the hearts of all the home economists hired to represent her, so they took the eyes of one person, the hair of another, and so on. A little stern, but certainly respected, she helped women stretch their war-time rations and was a soothing voice in her weekly radio show.

1955

Betty Gets Friendlier, Younger

Life was good to Betty—she grew younger, with a bigger smile and rounder face. The first-ever *Betty Crocker Picture Cookbook* was a bestseller, making her the First Lady of Food. Cooks of every level flocked for her recipes, which were always trustworthy, being well-tested in the Betty Crocker Kitchens. Her wise-yet-approachable style made her sought after for cooking and home management advice.

1965

Jackie O or Betty Crocker?

This 1965 portrait of Betty has her looking younger yet. Her stylish hair and attire are thought to look a little like former First Lady Jackie Kennedy, another well-loved woman of the age. Her red suit and pearls perfectly represented women of the day.

1969

A Bigger Role Outside the Home

Many people think this is a dead ringer for Mary Tyler Moore. Whether it was Betty's longer hair or her stylized suit and earrings, this portrait shows Betty changing with the times but, as always, dressed in red and white. She's more businesslike, symbolizing American women's increasingly significant role outside the home.

1972

Making Cooking Fun

With a hint of fun in Betty's face, her friendly, down-to-earth demeanor allowed cooks everywhere to learn to cook without the fear of having to be perfect. You can almost see a little gleam in her smile and twinkling blue eyes!

1980

Radiating Confidence

Betty chilled out a bit in the early '80s, with a more casual hairstyle and clothing. Women could identify with her and loved her friendly and approachable personality. As she constantly created new recipes that trended with the times, cooks knew they could count on them to work, satisfy their families and dazzle their friends.

"The First Lady of Food"

1986
Dressed to the 10s?

Depicting Betty as comfortable in the boardroom as much as she is in the kitchen, this portrait epitomized confidence. Did they go too far with this one? Those who work in the Betty Crocker Kitchens get a kick out of her bow in this portrait because it wouldn't be a good idea to wear it while standing over a hot stove!

1996
The Spirit of Betty

For her 75th birthday, a nationwide search was conducted to find 75 women of diverse backgrounds who embodied the spirit of Betty Crocker—women who enjoyed cooking and baking and were committed to family and friends, resourceful and creative in handling everyday tasks and involved in their communities. The resulting portrait reveals a Betty with a blend of many heritages—and also a change of eye color!

Favorite Quick Breads

Come fall, no one can seem to get enough pumpkin. Developed for the new *Betty Crocker Cookie Book* (2019), this recipe wins for the yummy ingredient combination . . . but most of all, for giving us permission to eat cookies for breakfast!

Pumpkin Bread Breakfast Cookies

PREP TIME: 30 Minutes | **START TO FINISH:** 55 Minutes | *About 1½ dozen cookies*

- ¾ cup chopped walnuts
- 1 cup butter, softened
- 1 cup granulated sugar
- ½ cup firmly packed brown sugar
- 1 cup canned pumpkin (from 15-oz can; not pumpkin pie mix)
- ¼ cup pure maple or maple-flavored syrup
- 1⅔ cups all-purpose flour
- 2 teaspoons pumpkin pie spice

- 1½ teaspoons ground cinnamon
- 1 teaspoon baking soda
- ½ teaspoon salt
- 2 cups old-fashioned or quick-cooking oats
- 1 cup sweetened dried cranberries
- ½ cup raw unsalted hulled pumpkin seeds (pepitas)

1 Heat oven to 350°F. Grease cookie sheets with shortening or cooking spray. Finely chop ½ cup of the walnuts. Set aside the remaining ¼ cup chopped walnuts and ½ cup finely chopped walnuts separately.

2 In large bowl, beat butter, granulated sugar and brown sugar with electric mixer on medium speed until blended. Add pumpkin and maple syrup; mix well. Beat in flour, pumpkin pie spice, cinnamon, baking soda and salt until well blended. Stir in oats, cranberries, pumpkin seeds and reserved ½ cup finely chopped walnuts; mix well.

3 On cookie sheets, drop batter by ¼-cupfuls 2 inches apart. Spread each cookie with metal spatula into 3-inch round. Sprinkle each cookie with about 1½ teaspoons of the reserved ¼ cup chopped walnuts.

4 Bake 15 to 17 minutes or until edges are set. Cool on cookie sheets 5 minutes; remove from cookie sheets to cooling racks. Cool completely, about 30 minutes.

1 COOKIE Calories 340; Total Fat 16g (Saturated Fat 7g, Trans Fat 0g); Cholesterol 25mg; Sodium 220mg; Total Carbohydrate 45g (Dietary Fiber 3g); Protein 4g **CARBOHYDRATE CHOICES:** 3

Betty's Kitchen Tips: Pepitas are actually pumpkin seeds without the hull, found only in specific types of pumpkins. They are available raw, roasted, salted and unsalted. Each type has a slightly different flavor, but all can be used for snacking, in salads, soups and main dishes and in cookies, breads and other baked goods.

Make Ahead: Keep these cookies on hand for breakfast on the run or snacking. Wrap each cookie individually in plastic wrap and freeze. Thaw frozen cookies about 15 minutes before serving.

How to Store: Store these cookies in tightly covered container in refrigerator or loosely covered at room temperature.

If you have to eat gluten free, you know how hard it is to find foods that actually taste great. We love this recipe that doesn't call for ingredients you can't pronounce in order to get delicious, homemade taste.

Gluten-Free Banana Bread Muffins

PREP TIME: 15 Minutes | **START TO FINISH:** 1 Hour 15 Minutes | *12 muffins*

1¾ cups almond flour

1 teaspoon ground cinnamon

¾ teaspoon baking soda

½ teaspoon salt

1½ cups mashed ripe bananas (3 medium bananas)

½ cup coconut oil, melted and cooled slightly

¼ cup pure maple syrup

1 teaspoon gluten-free vanilla

3 eggs, beaten

1 MUFFIN Calories 250; Total Fat 19g (Saturated Fat 9g, Trans Fat 0g); Cholesterol 45mg; Sodium 190mg; Total Carbohydrate 15g (Dietary Fiber 2g); Protein 5g **CARBOHYDRATE CHOICES:** 1

Cooking Gluten Free? Always read labels to make sure *each* recipe ingredient is gluten free. Products and ingredient sources can change.

Betty's Kitchen Tips: Use overripe bananas to maximize the banana flavor in these muffins.

How to Store: Store these moist muffins covered in the refrigerator up to 3 days.

1 Heat oven to 350°F. Place paper baking cup in each of 12 regular-size muffin cups.

2 In large bowl, mix almond flour, cinnamon, baking soda and salt. In another large bowl, mix bananas, oil, maple syrup, vanilla and eggs. Pour banana mixture into almond flour mixture; stir until just combined. Divide batter evenly among muffin cups (cups will be full).

3 Bake 22 to 27 minutes or until tops turn golden brown and until toothpick inserted in center comes out clean. Cool in pan 5 minutes; remove from pan to cooling rack. Cool completely, about 30 minutes.

RECITE

#3

Gluten-Free Chocolate-Zucchini Muffins

PREP TIME: 15 Minutes | **START TO FINISH:** 1 Hour 35 Minutes | *12 muffins*

- ½ cup coconut flour
- ½ cup unsweetened dark baking cocoa
- ½ teaspoon coarse (kosher or sea) salt
- ¼ teaspoon baking soda
- ½ cup coconut oil, melted and cooled slightly

- ½ cup pure maple syrup
- 1 teaspoon gluten-free vanilla
- About 1½ cups eggs (6 eggs)
- 1½ cups shredded zucchini
- ⅔ cup dark chocolate chips (70% cacao or higher)

1 MUFFIN Calories 250; Total Fat 16g (Saturated Fat 11g, Trans Fat 0g); Cholesterol 95mg; Sodium 160mg; Total Carbohydrate 21g (Dietary Fiber 2g); Protein 5g **CARBOHYDRATE CHOICES:** 1½

Cooking Gluten Free? Always read labels to make sure *each* recipe ingredient is gluten free. Products and ingredient sources can change.

How to Store: Store extra muffins at room temperature in a tightly covered container up to 2 days, or freeze up to 2 weeks.

1 Heat oven to 350°F. Place paper baking cup in each of 12 regular-size muffin cups.

2 In medium bowl, mix coconut flour, cocoa, salt and baking soda; set aside.

3 In large bowl, beat oil, syrup, vanilla and eggs with whisk. Stir in coconut flour mixture until blended. Stir in zucchini and chocolate chips. Divide batter evenly among muffin cups (cups will be full).

4 Bake 30 to 35 minutes or until toothpick inserted in center comes out clean. Cool in pan 10 minutes; remove from pan to cooling rack. Cool completely, about 30 minutes.

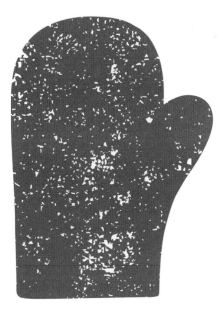

RECIPE #4

We've created a combo of two of our favorite pancakes into one for this special edition because we couldn't pick just one. A fine example of Betty's unending creativity and mission to whip up recipes that your family will devour!

Birthday Doughnut Pancakes

PREP TIME: 20 Minutes | START TO FINISH: 20 Minutes | *12 pancakes*

PANCAKES

- 2 cups Original Bisquick® mix
- ¾ cup milk
- 3 tablespoons candy sprinkles
- 1 tablespoon granulated sugar
- 1 teaspoon vanilla
- 2 eggs

GLAZE

- 1½ cups powdered sugar
- 3 tablespoons butter, melted
- 2 tablespoons milk
- 1 teaspoon vanilla
- 1 tablespoon candy sprinkles

1 PANCAKE Calories 210; Total Fat 7g (Saturated Fat 4g, Trans Fat 0g); Cholesterol 40mg; Sodium 230mg; Total Carbohydrate 33g (Dietary Fiber 0g); Protein 3g **CARBOHYDRATE CHOICES:** 2

COCOA GLAZED PANCAKES: Prepare glaze as directed—except stir 2 tablespoons unsweetened baking cocoa into powdered sugar. Stir in additional milk, 1 teaspoon at a time, until desired consistency.

MINI DOUGHNUT PANCAKES: Prepare as directed—except cut ¼ inch from corner of bag. For each doughnut pancake, squeeze batter into 2-inch circle.

1 Heat griddle to 375°F or 12-inch skillet over medium-high heat. (To test griddle, sprinkle with a few drops of water. If bubbles jump around, heat is just right.) Brush with vegetable oil if necessary.

2 In medium bowl, mix pancake ingredients with whisk or fork until blended. Place batter in gallon-size resealable food-storage plastic bag; cut ½ inch from bottom corner of bag.

3 For each pancake, squeeze batter from bag onto hot griddle into 4-inch circle, leaving hole in center. Cook 30 to 60 seconds or until bubbly on top and dry around edges. Turn; cook other side until dry around edges. Place on heatproof cooling rack on cookie sheet; cover loosely with foil and keep warm in 200°F oven while preparing remaining pancakes.

4 In small bowl, stir all glaze ingredients except sprinkles until smooth. Drizzle pancakes with glaze; sprinkle with sprinkles. Serve immediately.

RECIPE #5

Oatmeal Pancakes with Banana-Walnut Syrup

PREP TIME: 30 Minutes | START TO FINISH: 30 Minutes | *6 servings (3 pancakes each)*

BANANA-WALNUT SYRUP

- 2 tablespoons butter
- ¼ cup chopped walnuts
- 2 bananas, sliced
- 1 cup maple-flavored syrup

OATMEAL PANCAKES

- 2 cups Original Bisquick mix
- 1¼ cups milk
- ½ cup old-fashioned or quick-cooking oats
- 2 tablespoons packed brown sugar
- 2 eggs

1 SERVING Calories 500; Total Fat 13g (Saturated Fat 5g, Trans Fat 0g); Cholesterol 75mg; Sodium 490mg; Total Carbohydrate 86g (Dietary Fiber 3g); Protein 9g **CARBOHYDRATE CHOICES:** 6

1 In 1½-quart saucepan, melt butter over medium heat. Add walnuts; cook, stirring occasionally, until walnuts and butter just begin to brown. Add bananas; stir to coat with butter. Stir in syrup. Reduce heat to low; cook until warm. Keep syrup warm while making pancakes.

2 In medium bowl, mix oatmeal pancake ingredients with whisk or fork until blended.

3 Heat griddle to 375°F or 12-inch skillet over medium-high heat. (To test griddle, sprinkle with a few drops of water. If bubbles jump around, heat is just right.) Brush griddle with vegetable oil if necessary.

4 For each pancake, pour slightly less than ¼ cup batter onto hot griddle. Cook until edges are dry. Turn; cook other side until golden brown. Place on heatproof cooling rack on cookie sheet; cover loosely with foil and keep warm in 200°F oven while preparing remaining pancakes.

5 Serve pancakes with warm banana-walnut syrup.

CHOCOLATE CHIP PANCAKES: Prepare as directed—except omit banana-walnut syrup; omit oats and brown sugar. Increase milk to 2 cups. Stir ½ cup miniature chocolate chips into pancake batter. Cook pancakes as directed over medium (350°F) heat. Serve with maple-flavored syrup, if desired.

CANDIED GINGER–PUMPKIN PANCAKES: Prepare as directed—except omit banana-walnut syrup; omit oats, brown sugar and milk. Add 1½ cups buttermilk, 1 cup canned pumpkin (from 15-oz can; not pumpkin pie mix) and 2 teaspoons pumpkin pie spice with Bisquick mix. Stir ¼ cup finely chopped toasted pecans and 1 tablespoon finely chopped crystallized ginger into pancake batter. Cook pancakes as directed over medium (350°F) heat. Garnish pancakes with pecan halves and maple-flavored syrup, if desired.

Betty's Kitchen Tips: Pecans can be used instead of walnuts if you like.

Since 1931, Bisquick all-purpose baking mix has been helping home cooks get great-tasting recipes on the table. We can't resist the fresh, lemon-poppy seed combo paired with blueberry, as well as the clever way to make Belgian waffles without having to separate eggs. What a breakfast treat!

Lemon-Poppy Seed Belgian Waffles

PREP TIME: 30 Minutes | **START TO FINISH:** 30 Minutes | *12 servings (one 4-inch waffle and about 3 tablespoons syrup each)*

WAFFLES

- 2 cups Original Bisquick mix
- 1 to 2 tablespoons poppy seed
- 1 tablespoon grated lemon zest
- 1¼ cups cold club soda
- ¼ cup butter, melted
- 1 egg

BLUEBERRY-MAPLE SYRUP

- 1 bag (12 oz) frozen blueberries, thawed
- ½ cup pure maple or maple-flavored syrup
- 1 teaspoon grated lemon zest
- 2 teaspoons lemon juice

  Crème fraîche and additional lemon zest, if desired

1 In medium bowl, stir Bisquick mix, poppy seed and lemon zest. In small bowl, mix club soda, butter and egg with whisk; gently stir into Bisquick mixture with fork or whisk (mixture will be lumpy). Let stand 3 minutes.

2 Heat Belgian waffle maker; brush with vegetable oil. For each waffle, pour ¾ to 1 cup batter onto center of hot waffle maker. Close lid; bake about 5 minutes or until steaming stops and waffles are golden brown.

3 Meanwhile, in medium bowl, mix blueberries, maple syrup, lemon zest and lemon juice. Serve waffles with syrup, crème fraîche and additional lemon zest.

1 SERVING Calories 170; Total Fat 6g (Saturated Fat 3g, Trans Fat 0g); Cholesterol 25mg; Sodium 230mg; Total Carbohydrate 27g (Dietary Fiber 1g); Protein 2g **CARBOHYDRATE CHOICES:** 2

This recipe makes the grade for the creative combination of ingredients that take waffles into a savory realm—yum! Betty's always looking for new ways to take ingredients you love and turn them into recipes that will bring raves.

Bacon, Corn and Hash Brown Waffles

PREP TIME: 30 Minutes | START TO FINISH: 30 Minutes | *5 waffles*

3 eggs
6 cups frozen shredded hash brown potatoes (from 30-oz bag), thawed
1 cup shredded cheddar cheese
½ cup Original Bisquick mix
½ cup chopped crisply cooked bacon (about 8 slices)
½ cup frozen corn kernels, thawed

¼ cup milk
2 tablespoons finely chopped green onion
½ teaspoon salt
¾ cup chive-and-onion sour cream potato topper (from 12-oz container)
Additional chopped crisply cooked bacon and chopped green onion, if desired

1 Brush waffle maker with vegetable oil or spray with cooking spray. Heat waffle maker.

2 In large bowl, beat eggs with whisk until fluffy. Stir in potatoes, cheese, Bisquick mix, bacon, corn, milk, green onion and salt until well mixed.

3 Scoop about 1 cup of waffle mixture onto center of hot waffle maker; spread slightly. Close lid of waffle maker.

4 Bake 2 to 3 minutes or until waffle is golden brown. Carefully remove waffle to cooling rack; repeat with remaining batter. Serve topped with dollop of potato topper and additional bacon and green onion.

1 WAFFLE Calories 530; Total Fat 21g (Saturated Fat 11g, Trans Fat 0g); Cholesterol 165mg; Sodium 870mg; Total Carbohydrate 66g (Dietary Fiber 6g); Protein 19g **CARBOHYDRATE CHOICES:** 4½

Betty's Kitchen Tips: To quickly thaw frozen hash brown potatoes, place in large microwavable bowl. Microwave uncovered on High for 3 to 4 minutes, stirring after each minute and breaking up large pieces with spoon.

A Puzzle and Pin Cushion Started It All

The puzzle and pin cushion that caused Betty's birth! The puzzle came in sacks of Gold Medal flour in 1921. If you cut it apart, put it together correctly and sent it in, you'd get a miniature flour sack-shaped pin cushion. Hundreds of consumers sent in the completed puzzles . . . and with them, questions about cooking and baking. So then Betty Crocker was born to answer the consumer questions and to be a helpful resource in the kitchen.

> "This is the most requested blueberry recipe that I make every year. Nobody wants to share the cake, even with their spouse. I have already baked eight cakes this year and have only been able to eat two pieces myself." Need we say more?

Blueberry Best Coffee Cake

PREP TIME: 25 Minutes | **START TO FINISH:** 1 Hour 25 Minutes | *9 servings*

CRUMB TOPPING
- ½ cup granulated sugar
- ⅓ cup all-purpose flour
- ½ teaspoon ground cinnamon
- ¼ cup butter, softened

COFFEE CAKE
- 2 cups all-purpose flour
- ¾ cup granulated sugar
- ¾ cup milk
- ¼ cup shortening
- 2½ teaspoons baking powder
- ¾ teaspoon salt
- 1 egg
- 2 cups fresh or frozen blueberries (do not thaw)

VANILLA GLAZE
- ½ cup powdered sugar
- 1 to 1½ teaspoons hot water
- ¼ teaspoon vanilla

1 Heat oven to 375°F. Grease bottom and side of 9-inch springform pan or 9-inch square pan with shortening or cooking spray.

2 In small bowl, mix sugar, flour and cinnamon. Cut in butter with fork until crumbly. Set aside.

3 In large bowl, mix all coffee cake ingredients except blueberries; beat with spoon 30 seconds. Fold in blueberries. Spread batter in pan. Sprinkle with crumb topping.

4 Bake 45 to 50 minutes or until toothpick inserted in center comes out clean. Cool in pan 10 minutes; remove side of pan.

5 In small bowl, mix glaze ingredients until smooth and thin enough to drizzle. Drizzle over warm coffee cake.

1 SERVING Calories 390; Total Fat 12g (Saturated Fat 5g, Trans Fat 0g); Cholesterol 35mg; Sodium 390mg; Total Carbohydrate 65g (Dietary Fiber 2g); Protein 5g **CARBOHYDRATE CHOICES:** 4

CRAN-RASPBERRY COFFEE CAKE: Prepare as directed—except substitute 1 cup fresh or frozen raspberries and 1 cup fresh or frozen cranberries, cut in half, for the blueberries.

How to Store: Tightly wrap and refrigerate for 1 week or freeze up to 6 months.

It's always good to have a great coffee cake in your back pocket for when you want to have a special breakfast or brunch: "So many compliments. This is a keeper!!!!"

Blackberry Coffee Cake

PREP TIME: 25 Minutes | START TO FINISH: 3 Hours 10 Minutes | *16 servings*

FILLING

1¼ cups frozen blackberries, thawed and well drained
½ cup finely chopped pecans
3 tablespoons granulated sugar
1½ teaspoons ground cinnamon

COFFEE CAKE

2¼ cups all-purpose flour
1 teaspoon baking powder
½ teaspoon baking soda
1¼ cups granulated sugar
1 cup butter, softened
1 teaspoon vanilla
2 eggs
1 container (8 oz) sour cream

GLAZE

1½ cups powdered sugar
3 to 4 teaspoons water

1 Heat oven to 350°F. Grease bottom and side of 10-inch angel food (tube) cake pan with shortening or spray with cooking spray; lightly flour.

2 In small bowl, mix filling ingredients; set aside.

3 In medium bowl, mix flour, baking powder and baking soda; set aside. In large bowl, beat granulated sugar, butter, vanilla and eggs with electric mixer on medium speed 2 minutes, scraping bowl occasionally. On low speed, alternately add flour mixture with sour cream, beating after each addition, just until blended.

4 Spread one-third of batter in pan; sprinkle with half of filling. Spoon another one-third of batter by tablespoonfuls over filling; sprinkle with remaining filling. Spoon remaining batter over filling; spread evenly.

5 Bake 55 to 65 minutes or until toothpick inserted in center of cake comes out clean. Cool in pan 10 minutes; remove from pan to cooling rack. Cool completely, about 1 hour 30 minutes.

6 In small bowl, mix glaze ingredients until smooth and thin enough to drizzle. Drizzle glaze over coffee cake.

1 SERVING Calories 360; Total Fat 18g (Saturated Fat 9g, Trans Fat 0.5g); Cholesterol 60mg; Sodium 190mg; Total Carbohydrate 46g (Dietary Fiber 1g); Protein 3g **CARBOHYDRATE CHOICES:** 3

Make Ahead: Wrap unglazed coffee cake tightly and freeze up to 2 months. Thaw and drizzle with glaze just before serving.

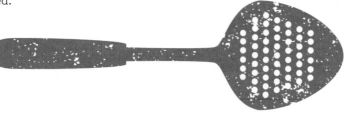

Is it a breakfast bread or is it dessert? The nutty brown sugar streusel makes it a winner, either way. "I made this for a group event and everybody raved about it! Big hit."

Mocha Streusel Coffee Cake

PREP TIME: 25 Minutes | START TO FINISH: 2 Hours 30 Minutes | *12 servings*

STREUSEL

- ⅔ cup miniature semisweet chocolate chips
- ½ cup chopped pecans
- ⅓ cup packed brown sugar
- 2 tablespoons all-purpose flour
- 1 tablespoon instant coffee granules or crystals

COFFEE CAKE

- 2¾ cups all-purpose flour
- 2 teaspoons baking powder
- 1 teaspoon ground cinnamon
- ¼ teaspoon baking soda
- ¼ teaspoon salt
- 1 cup granulated sugar
- 1 cup butter, softened
- ½ teaspoon almond extract
- 3 eggs
- 1 container (8 oz) sour cream

1 Heat oven to 350°F. Grease bottom and side of 10-inch angel food (tube) cake pan with shortening or spray with cooking spray.

2 In small bowl, mix streusel ingredients; set aside.

3 In medium bowl, mix flour, baking powder, cinnamon, baking soda and salt. In large bowl, beat granulated sugar and butter with electric mixer on medium speed until light and fluffy. Beat in almond extract. Add eggs one at a time, beating well after each addition. Add half of the flour mixture; beat on low speed just until combined. Beat in sour cream until well blended. Beat in remaining flour mixture.

4 Spoon half of the batter into pan; spread evenly. Sprinkle with half of the streusel. Repeat with remaining batter and streusel.

5 Bake 55 to 65 minutes or until toothpick inserted in center of cake comes out clean. Cool in pan on cooling rack 1 hour. Remove cake from pan.

1 SERVING Calories 480; Total Fat 27g (Saturated Fat 14g, Trans Fat 0.5g); Cholesterol 95mg; Sodium 310mg; Total Carbohydrate 54g (Dietary Fiber 2g); Protein 6g **CARBOHYDRATE CHOICES:** 3½

How to Store: Cool baked coffee cake completely. Wrap the cake tightly and refrigerate up to 1 week or freeze up to 2 months.

The original recipe was one of the first recipes our executive editor ever created in the Betty Crocker Kitchens. It was supposed to be a muffin without the pan. When she saw the results, she realized that while it wasn't a muffin, a glaze could be added and it was an easy way to make Danish! And it still remains a popular recipe today.

Easy Drop Danish

PREP TIME: 10 Minutes | **START TO FINISH:** 25 Minutes | *12 Danish*

2 cups Original Bisquick mix

¼ cup butter, softened

2 tablespoons granulated sugar

⅔ cup milk

¼ cup raspberry preserves (or other flavor)

VANILLA GLAZE

¾ cup powdered sugar

1 tablespoon milk

¼ teaspoon vanilla

1 DANISH Calories 170; Total Fat 6g (Saturated Fat 3g, Trans Fat 0g); Cholesterol 10mg; Sodium 230mg; Total Carbohydrate 29g (Dietary Fiber 0g); Protein 2g **CARBOHYDRATE CHOICES:** 2

EASY CHEESE DROP DANISH: Prepare as directed—except omit preserves. In small bowl, mix 3 oz softened cream cheese, 1 tablespoon granulated sugar and 1 tablespoon milk. Fill wells with cream cheese mixture in Step 2. Bake 8 to 10 minutes or until golden brown.

1 Heat oven to 450°F. Grease cookie sheet with shortening or cooking spray.

2 In medium bowl, mix Bisquick mix, butter and granulated sugar until crumbly. Stir in milk until dough forms; beat 15 strokes. On cookie sheet, drop dough by rounded tablespoonfuls about 2 inches apart. Make shallow well in center of each with back of spoon; fill with 1 teaspoon preserves.

3 Bake 10 to 15 minutes or until golden brown.

4 In small bowl, mix vanilla glaze ingredients. Drizzle over warm Danish.

RECIPE

#12

Banana Bread

PREP TIME: 15 Minutes | START TO FINISH: 3 Hours 40 Minutes | *2 loaves (12 slices each)*

1¼ cups sugar
½ cup butter, softened
2 eggs
1½ cups mashed very ripe bananas (3 medium)
½ cup buttermilk
1 teaspoon vanilla

2½ cups all-purpose flour
1 teaspoon baking soda
1 teaspoon salt
1 cup chopped nuts, if desired

1 Heat oven to 350°F. Grease bottoms only of 2 (8×4- or 9×5-inch) loaf pans with shortening or cooking spray.

2 In large bowl, stir sugar and butter until well mixed. Stir in eggs until well mixed. Stir in bananas, buttermilk and vanilla; beat with spoon until smooth. Stir in flour, baking soda and salt just until moistened. Stir in nuts. Divide batter evenly between pans.

3 Bake 8-inch loaves about 1 hour, 9-inch loaves about 1 hour 15 minutes, or until toothpick inserted in center comes out clean. Cool in pans 10 minutes on cooling rack.

4 Loosen sides of loaves from pans; remove from pans and place, top side up, on cooling rack. Cool completely, about 2 hours, before slicing.

1 SLICE Calories 150; Total Fat 4.5g (Saturated Fat 2.5g, Trans Fat 0g); Cholesterol 30mg; Sodium 190mg; Total Carbohydrate 24g (Dietary Fiber 0g); Protein 2g **CARBOHYDRATE CHOICES:** 1½

STRAWBERRY-BANANA BREAD: Prepare as directed—except substitute 1 cup chopped fresh strawberries for nuts.

BANANA–CHOCOLATE CHIP LOAF: Prepare as directed—except substitute semisweet or milk chocolate chips for nuts.

BLUEBERRY-BANANA BREAD: Prepare as directed—except substitute 1 cup fresh or frozen (do not thaw) blueberries for nuts.

APRICOT-BANANA BREAD: Prepare as directed—except stir 1 cup chopped dried apricots in with nuts. Use chopped pecans for nuts.

CRANBERRY ORANGE BANANA BREAD: Prepare as directed—except add ¼ cup grated orange zest (from 2 large oranges) with bananas. Substitute ½ cup dried sweetened cranberries for ½ cup of the nuts. When loaves are cool, mix 1 cup powdered sugar and enough orange juice (4 to 6 tablespoons) until smooth and drizzling consistency. Drizzle over loaves. Let glaze set before wrapping and storing.

Betty's Kitchen Tips: No buttermilk? No problem! Place 1½ teaspoons lemon juice or vinegar in a measuring cup; add enough milk to equal ½ cup.

Continues

Strawberry–
Banana Bread

Banana Bread *continued*

Betty's Kitchen Tips: A serrated knife, used with a light sawing motion, works best for cutting nice slices.

Betty's Kitchen Tips: The banana flavor is even better when loaves have been refrigerated 24 hours.

How to Store: Wrap completely cooled loaves tightly in plastic wrap or foil and store at room temperature 4 days or refrigerate up to 1 week. For longer storage, place wrapped loaves in freezer plastic bags and freeze up to 3 months.

Strawberry-
Banana Bread

In our 1950 *Betty Crocker Picture Cookbook,* we included a recipe for White Nut Loaf, with variations for Fig or Date Nut Loaf. For our ever-increasingly sophisticated taste buds, this quick bread includes two of today's favorites—pumpkin and chocolate.

Pumpkin-Chocolate Chip Bread

PREP TIME: 25 Minutes | START TO FINISH: 4 Hours 10 Minutes | *1 loaf (16 slices)*

BREAD
- 1 cup granulated sugar
- 1 cup canned pumpkin (from 15-oz can; not pumpkin pie mix)
- ½ cup butter, softened
- 2 eggs
- 2 cups all-purpose flour
- 1 teaspoon baking soda
- 1 teaspoon ground cinnamon
- 1 teaspoon pumpkin pie spice
- ½ cup miniature semisweet chocolate chips
- ¼ cup chopped walnuts

GLAZE
- ½ cup powdered sugar
- 2 to 3 teaspoons milk or whipping cream

1 Heat oven to 350°F. Grease bottom only of 9×5-inch loaf pan with shortening or cooking spray.

2 In large bowl, mix granulated sugar, pumpkin, butter and eggs with wire whisk. Stir in flour, baking soda, cinnamon and pumpkin pie spice. Stir in chocolate chips and walnuts. Spread in pan.

3 Bake 55 to 65 minutes or until toothpick inserted in center comes out clean. Cool in pan 10 minutes; remove from pan to cooling rack. Cool completely, about 2 hours.

4 In small bowl, mix glaze ingredients until smooth and thin enough to drizzle. Drizzle over top of loaf. Let glaze set about 30 minutes before slicing.

1 SLICE Calories 230; Total Fat 9g (Saturated Fat 5g, Trans Fat 0g); Cholesterol 40mg; Sodium 130mg; Total Carbohydrate 33g (Dietary Fiber 1g); Protein 3g **CARBOHYDRATE CHOICES:** 2

PUMPKIN-CRANBERRY BREAD: Substitute sweetened dried cranberries for the chocolate chips.

This recipe delivers on flavor and texture, while having 50% less fat, 21% fewer calories and 2g more fiber than the original recipe. "This was not only healthy but also tasted good. Froze one loaf but my husband is already asking for it."

Skinny Zucchini Bread

PREP TIME: 25 Minutes | **START TO FINISH:** 2 Hours 35 Minutes | *2 loaves (12 slices each)*

2½ cups shredded zucchini (about 2 medium)

1½ cups sugar

1 cup unsweetened applesauce

¾ cup fat-free egg product or 3 eggs

½ cup canola oil

2 teaspoons vanilla

1½ cups all-purpose flour

1½ cups whole wheat flour

3 teaspoons ground cinnamon

1 teaspoon baking soda

1 teaspoon salt

¼ teaspoon baking powder

½ cup chopped walnuts or pecans

1 Heat oven to 350°F. Grease bottoms only of 2 (8×4-inch) loaf pans with shortening or cooking spray.

2 In large bowl, mix zucchini, sugar, applesauce, egg product, oil and vanilla until well blended. Stir in all remaining ingredients except walnuts until well blended. Stir in walnuts. Spoon batter evenly into pans.

3 Bake 50 to 60 minutes or until toothpick inserted in center comes out clean. Cool in pans 10 minutes. Loosen sides of loaves from pans; remove from pans to cooling racks. Cool completely, about 1 hour.

1 SLICE Calories 180; Total Fat 6g (Saturated Fat 0.5g, Trans Fat 0g); Cholesterol 0mg; Sodium 170mg; Total Carbohydrate 26g (Dietary Fiber 1g); Protein 3g **CARBOHYDRATE CHOICES:** 2

In the 1956 *Betty Crocker Picture Cookbook,* a recipe for Quick Apple Cake gave directions to arrange apple slices on top of the coffee cake and sprinkle cinnamon-sugar over them. We've updated this recipe by grating the apple and adding pecans, cinnamon and nutmeg to the bread, then topping it with an irresistible caramel glaze.

Caramel-Glazed Apple Bread

PREP TIME: 20 Minutes | START TO FINISH: 2 Hours 55 Minutes | *2 loaves (12 slices each)*

BREAD

- 1½ cups shredded peeled baking apples (2 large)
- 1 cup packed brown sugar
- ½ cup buttermilk
- ½ cup vegetable oil
- 4 eggs, lightly beaten
- 3 cups all-purpose flour
- ½ cup chopped pecans
- 2 teaspoons baking soda
- 2 teaspoons ground cinnamon
- 1 teaspoon salt
- 1 teaspoon ground nutmeg

CARAMEL GLAZE

- 2 tablespoons butter
- ¼ cup packed brown sugar
- 1 tablespoon milk
- ½ cup powdered sugar

1 Heat oven to 350°F. Grease bottoms only of 2 (8×4-inch) loaf pans with shortening or cooking spray.

2 In large bowl, mix apples, brown sugar, buttermilk, oil and eggs. Stir in remaining bread ingredients just until dry ingredients are moistened. Spread batter evenly into pans.

3 Bake 45 to 55 minutes or until toothpick inserted in center comes out clean. Cool in pans 10 minutes on cooling rack. Loosen sides of loaves from pans; remove from pans and place on cooling rack top sides up. Cool completely, about 1 hour.

4 In 1-quart saucepan, melt butter over medium heat. Stir in brown sugar. Heat to boiling, stirring constantly; reduce heat to low. Boil and stir 2 minutes. Stir in milk. Heat to boiling; remove from heat. Cool to lukewarm, about 30 minutes.

5 Gradually stir powdered sugar into glaze mixture. Place saucepan of glaze in bowl of cold water. Beat with spoon until smooth and thin enough to drizzle. If glaze becomes too stiff, stir in additional milk, ½ teaspoon at a time, or heat over low heat, stirring constantly. Drizzle glaze over tops of loaves.

1 SLICE Calories 200; Total Fat 8g (Saturated Fat 2g, Trans Fat 0g); Cholesterol 35mg; Sodium 230mg; Total Carbohydrate 29g (Dietary Fiber 1g); Protein 3g **CARBOHYDRATE CHOICES:** 2

How to Store: Wrap glazed loaves tightly and store at room temperature up to 4 days or refrigerate up to 10 days.

It's the best of old and new! We've matched our best cake doughnut with a fun, contemporary glaze. "I had a Betty Crocker cookbook in the '70s, and I loved this recipe. I no longer have the book and am so happy to have found this recipe again! They are delicious!"

Cake Doughnuts with Rainbow Glaze

PREP TIME: 45 Minutes | START TO FINISH: 1 Hour 15 Minutes | *24 doughnuts*

DOUGHNUTS
Vegetable oil
3⅓ cups all-purpose flour
1 cup granulated sugar
¾ cup milk
3 teaspoons baking powder
½ teaspoon salt
½ teaspoon ground cinnamon
¼ teaspoon ground nutmeg
2 tablespoons shortening
2 eggs

RAINBOW GLAZE
4½ cups powdered sugar
6 tablespoons milk
¼ cup light corn syrup
Red, orange, yellow, green, blue and purple gel icing colors (not liquid food color)

1 In large bowl, beat 1½ cups of the flour and the remaining doughnut ingredients with electric mixer on low speed 30 seconds, scraping bowl constantly. Beat on medium speed 2 minutes, scraping bowl occasionally. Stir in remaining flour until well mixed.

2 On generously floured surface, roll dough lightly to coat in flour. Gently roll out to ⅜-inch thickness. With floured 2½-inch doughnut cutter, cut dough into 24 rounds, rerolling dough if necessary.

3 In deep fryer or 3-quart saucepan, heat 3 to 4 inches oil to 375°F.

4 Fry doughnuts and doughnut holes in oil, 2 to 3 at a time. Turn as they rise to the surface; fry 2 to 3 minutes longer or until golden brown on both sides. Remove from oil with slotted spoon; drain on paper towels.

5 In large bowl, mix all rainbow glaze ingredients except gel colors until smooth. Divide evenly among 6 small bowls. Add a different color gel to each bowl; stir to blend. Place each color glaze in small resealable food-storage plastic bag. Cut off tiny corner of each bag.

6 Place cooling rack on large cookie sheet; place doughnuts on rack. To make a rainbow on each doughnut, pipe one stripe each of red, orange, yellow, green, blue and purple glaze over top and slightly over edge of doughnut so colors just touch. The glaze will spread slightly and drip down side. Glaze 1 or 2 doughnuts at a time with all colors so glaze can blend together slightly before setting. Frost doughnut holes with remaining glaze. Let stand at least 30 minutes or until glaze is set.

1 DOUGHNUT Calories 300; Total Fat 11g (Saturated Fat 2g, Trans Fat 0g); Cholesterol 15mg; Sodium 125mg; Total Carbohydrate 48g (Dietary Fiber 0g); Protein 2g **CARBOHYDRATE CHOICES:** 3

BUTTERMILK DOUGHNUTS: Prepare as directed—except substitute buttermilk for milk, decrease baking powder to 2 teaspoons and add 1 teaspoon baking soda.

Betty's Kitchen Tips: The glaze may seem thick at first, but don't be tempted to thin it. It will flow just enough to drip slightly down side of doughnut. If it is too thin, it will not set up and will run off the doughnut.

How to Store: Store glazed doughnuts in a tightly covered container.

Doughnuts you don't have to fry, flavored with the fresh, citrusy flavor of orange as well as blueberries and with a streusel topping. That's a winner every time!

Baked Blueberry-Orange Doughnuts

PREP TIME: 25 Minutes | START TO FINISH: 40 Minutes | *12 doughnuts*

STREUSEL
- 3 tablespoons all-purpose flour
- 3 tablespoons sugar
- 1 tablespoon butter
- 3 tablespoons sliced almonds
- ½ teaspoon grated orange zest

DOUGHNUTS
- ⅔ cup sugar
- ½ cup butter, softened
- 2 eggs
- ¼ cup milk
- 2 teaspoons grated orange zest
- ¼ cup fresh orange juice
- 2 cups all-purpose flour
- 1½ teaspoons baking powder
- ½ teaspoon salt
- ¾ cup fresh blueberries

1 Heat oven to 425°F. Lightly spray 2 regular-size doughnut pans (6 doughnuts per pan) with cooking spray.

2 In small bowl, mix flour and sugar. Cut in butter, using pastry blender or fork, until mixture is crumbly. Stir in remaining streusel ingredients; set aside.

3 In medium bowl, beat sugar, butter and eggs with electric mixer on medium speed until smooth.

Add milk and orange juice; beat on low speed until well mixed. Stir in flour, orange zest, baking powder and salt just until flour is moistened. Fold in blueberries.

4 Spoon batter evenly into doughnut pans, filling wells about ¼ inch from top of pan; sprinkle with streusel. Bake 6 to 8 minutes or until toothpick inserted in center comes out clean. Cool in pans 5 minutes; remove from pans to cooling rack. Serve warm or cool.

1 DOUGHNUT Calories 250; Total Fat 11g (Saturated Fat 6g, Trans Fat 0g); Cholesterol 55mg; Sodium 250mg; Total Carbohydrate 34g (Dietary Fiber 1g); Protein 4g **CARBOHYDRATE CHOICES:** 2

Betty's Kitchen Tips: Small blueberries work best for this recipe so you will get berries in each doughnut.

Make Ahead: Cool doughnuts completely. Wrap tightly. Freeze up to 3 months. Thaw loosely covered at room temperature.

Garlic-Cheese
Biscuits

Baking Powder Biscuits never go out of style, and have been around since our first cookbook. Over time, people have also fallen in love with our Bisquick mix recipe and our restaurant-style garlic-cheese variation. You'll find both recipes here for you, no matter which one you want to make!

Baking Powder Biscuits

PREP TIME: 10 Minutes | **START TO FINISH:** 25 Minutes | *12 biscuits*

2 cups all-purpose flour
1 tablespoon sugar
1 tablespoon baking powder
1 teaspoon salt
½ cup shortening or cold butter, cut into 8 pieces
¾ cup milk

1 Heat oven to 450°F.

2 In medium bowl, mix flour, sugar, baking powder and salt. Cut in shortening, using pastry blender or fork, until mixture looks like fine crumbs. Stir in milk until dough leaves side of bowl.

3 On lightly floured surface, lightly knead dough 10 times. Roll or pat until ½-inch thick. With floured 2- to 2¼-inch biscuit cutter, cut dough into rounds, rerolling if necessary. On ungreased cookie sheet, place biscuits about 1 inch apart for crusty sides, touching for soft sides.

4 Bake 10 to 12 minutes or until golden brown. Immediately remove from cookie sheet to cooling rack. Serve warm.

1 BISCUIT Calories 160; Total Fat 9g (Saturated Fat 2.5g, Trans Fat 1.5g); Cholesterol 0mg; Sodium 330mg; Total Carbohydrate 18g (Dietary Fiber 0g); Protein 2g **CARBOHYDRATE CHOICES:** 1

DROP BISCUITS: Prepare as directed—except increase milk to 1 cup. Grease cookie sheet with shortening or cooking spray. On cookie sheet, drop 12 spoonfuls dough about 2 inches apart.

EASY BISQUICK BISCUITS: Prepare as directed—except substitute 2¼ cups Original Bisquick mix for flour. Omit sugar, baking powder, salt and shortening. Reduce milk to ⅔ cup. Stir until soft dough forms. Substitute Bisquick for flour in Step 3; proceed with step as directed. Bake biscuits 8 to 10 minutes. For drop biscuits: Drop dough by 9 spoonfuls on cookie sheet.

GARLIC-CHEESE BISCUITS: Prepare Easy Bisquick Biscuits as directed—except add ½ cup shredded cheddar cheese with milk. Mix 2 tablespoons melted butter and ⅛ teaspoon garlic powder; brush over warm biscuits.

Betty's Kitchen Tips: Stir only until the dough leaves side of bowl, as mixing too much can cause biscuits to be low volume and tough. Be sure to remove biscuits from cookie sheet to cooling rack immediately after baking to avoid them sticking to pan.

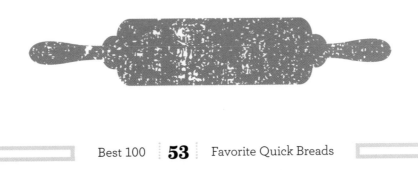

Our 1950 recipe had this in the introduction: "used by hunters and traders on their long journeys on foot . . . hence, the name 'Journey Cake,' later 'Johnny Cake.'" Created for *Betty Crocker The Big Book of Bread,* this recipe resembles some of our favorite restaurant cornbread.

Beer and Chile Cornbread Muffins

PREP TIME: 15 Minutes | START TO FINISH: 40 Minutes | *12 muffins*

2   eggs
1   cup Mexican or
     domestic beer
¼   cup butter, melted
¾   cup all-purpose flour
¾   cup yellow or blue
     cornmeal
½   cup sugar
½   cup shredded
     cheddar–Monterey
     Jack cheese blend
     (2 oz)

½   cup vacuum-packed
     whole kernel corn
     (from 11-oz can)
2   teaspoons baking
     powder
½   teaspoon salt
1   medium (5-inch)
     poblano chile,
     seeded, chopped
1   serrano chile, seeded,
     finely chopped

1 MUFFIN Calories 180; Total Fat 6g (Saturated Fat 3.5g, Trans Fat 0g); Cholesterol 50mg; Sodium 260mg; Total Carbohydrate 25g (Dietary Fiber 1g); Protein 4g **CARBOHYDRATE CHOICES:** 1½

Betty's Kitchen Tips: Poblano chiles are large and fairly mild in flavor. They add a delicious, fresh taste to these cornbread muffins.

1 Heat oven to 400°F. Place paper baking cup in each of 12 regular-size muffin cups, or grease bottoms only with shortening.

2 In medium bowl, beat eggs with fork. Stir in beer and butter. Stir in remaining ingredients all at once just until flour is moistened (batter will be lumpy). Divide batter evenly among muffin cups (cups will be full).

3 Bake 15 to 20 minutes or until golden brown and toothpick inserted in center comes out clean. Cool in pan 3 minutes; remove muffins from pan to cooling rack. Serve warm.

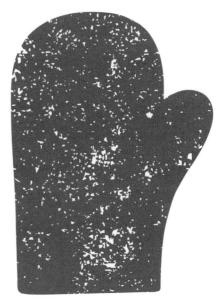

"High hat muffins, popped so they are crusty shells, hollow inside" is how popovers were described in our first *Betty Crocker Picture Cookbook*—and they are still adored for their fun texture (and for slathering with honey-butter). Betty Crocker has been demystifying popovers for generations of cooks with this easy-to-follow recipe.

Popovers

PREP TIME: 10 Minutes | START TO FINISH: 45 Minutes | *6 popovers*

2 eggs
1 cup all-purpose flour

1 cup milk
½ teaspoon salt

1 POPOVER Calories 120; Total Fat 3g (Saturated Fat 1g, Trans Fat 0g); Cholesterol 65mg; Sodium 240mg; Total Carbohydrate 18g (Dietary Fiber 0g); Protein 5g **CARBOHYDRATE CHOICES:** 1

1 Heat oven to 450°F. Generously grease 6-cup popover pan with shortening. Heat popover pan in oven 5 minutes.

2 Meanwhile, in medium bowl, beat eggs slightly with fork or whisk. Beat in remaining ingredients just until smooth (do not overbeat or popovers may not puff as high). Fill cups about half full.

3 Bake 20 minutes. Reduce oven temperature to 325°F. Bake 10 to 15 minutes longer or until deep golden brown. Immediately pierce with tip of paring knife and remove from cups. Serve hot.

Betty's Kitchen Tips: Make your popovers really high with these tips: Heat pan in oven; mix batter just until smooth, then quickly pour in batter.

Betty's Kitchen Tips: Keep your popovers from deflating by generously greasing interior as well as lip of each popover cup. Immediately after baking, pierce tops of popovers in a few places with tip of paring knife so steam can escape and remove from pan.

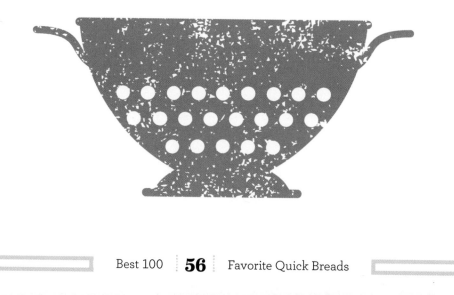

Best
Yeast
Breads

RECITE #21

Our cinnamon roll recipes date back to our first cookbook, which called for compressed yeast and made 18 rolls. We've updated our recipe for today's active dry yeast, adjusting ingredients and methods to get the yummiest results. We've also reduced the yield to 12, making them bigger, like you'd get in a bakery. You're welcome!

Jumbo Cinnamon Rolls

PREP TIME: 30 Minutes | START TO FINISH: 3 Hours 15 Minutes | *12 rolls*

ROLLS
- 3½ to 4 cups all-purpose or bread flour
- ⅓ cup granulated sugar
- 1 teaspoon salt
- 2 packages regular active or fast-acting dry yeast (4½ teaspoons)
- 1 cup very warm milk (120°F to 130°F)
- ¼ cup butter, softened
- 1 egg

FILLING
- ¼ cup granulated sugar
- 1 teaspoon ground cinnamon
- 2 tablespoons butter, softened

FROSTING
- 3 oz cream cheese (from 8-oz package), softened
- ¼ cup butter, softened
- 1½ cups powdered sugar
- ½ teaspoon vanilla

1 In large bowl, mix 2 cups of the flour, the granulated sugar, salt and yeast. Add milk, ¼ cup butter and the egg. Beat with electric mixer on low speed 1 minute, scraping bowl frequently. Beat on medium speed 1 minute, scraping bowl frequently. Stir in enough remaining flour, ½ cup at a time, to make dough easy to handle.

2 Place dough on lightly floured surface. Knead about 5 minutes or until dough is smooth and springy. Grease large bowl with shortening. Place dough in bowl, turning dough to grease all sides. Cover bowl loosely with plastic wrap and let rise in warm place about 1 hour 30 minutes or until dough has doubled in size. Dough is ready if indentation remains when touched.

3 Meanwhile, in small bowl, mix granulated sugar and cinnamon; set aside. Grease bottom and sides of 13×9-inch pan with shortening or cooking spray.

4 Gently push fist into dough to deflate. On lightly floured surface, flatten dough with hands or rolling pin into 15×10-inch rectangle. Spread with 2 tablespoons butter; sprinkle with cinnamon-sugar. Roll rectangle up tightly, beginning at 15-inch side. Pinch edge of dough into roll to seal. With fingers, shape roll until evenly round. With dental floss or serrated knife, cut roll into 12 (1¼-inch) slices.

5 Place slices slightly apart in pan, cut sides down. Cover loosely with plastic wrap and let rise in warm place about 1 hour or until slices have doubled in size.

6 Meanwhile, heat oven to 350°F.

7 Remove plastic wrap. Bake 28 to 33 minutes or until golden brown. Cool in pan 10 minutes on cooling rack.

8 Meanwhile, in medium bowl, beat frosting ingredients with electric mixer on medium speed until smooth and spreadable.

9 Spread frosting on rolls; serve warm.

1 ROLL Calories 360; Total Fat 13g (Saturated Fat 8g, Trans Fat 0g); Cholesterol 50mg; Sodium 310mg; Total Carbohydrate 55g (Dietary Fiber 1g); Protein 6g **CARBOHYDRATE CHOICES:** 3½

Continues

Jumbo Cinnamon Rolls continued

CARAMEL STICKY ROLLS: Prepare as directed—except while dough is rising in Step 2, in 2-quart saucepan, heat 1 cup packed brown sugar and ½ cup softened butter to boiling, stirring constantly; remove from heat. Stir in ¼ cup light corn syrup. Pour into ungreased 13×9-inch pan. Sprinkle with 1 cup pecan halves. In Step 3, substitute ¼ cup packed brown sugar for granulated sugar in filling. After baking, let rolls stand 2 to 3 minutes. Place heatproof plate upside down over pan; turn plate and pan over together. Let stand 1 minute so caramel can drizzle over rolls; remove pan. Omit frosting.

Make Ahead: After placing slices in pan, cover tightly with plastic wrap or foil; refrigerate 4 to 24 hours. About 2½ hours before serving, remove from refrigerator. Remove plastic wrap or foil and cover loosely with clean plastic wrap. Let rise in warm place until slices have doubled in size. If some rising occurred in refrigerator, this rising time may be less than 2 hours. Bake and frost as directed.

Originally created for the *Betty Crocker Baking Basics* cookbook, this old-fashioned favorite is hard to beat. If food were a love letter, this would be Betty's letter to us!

Monkey Bread

PREP TIME: 35 Minutes | START TO FINISH: 3 Hours 25 Minutes | *16 servings*

3½ to 4 cups all-purpose flour

⅓ cup sugar

1 teaspoon salt

1 package regular active or fast-acting dry yeast (2¼ teaspoons)

1 cup water

⅓ cup butter, softened

1 egg

¾ cup sugar

½ cup finely chopped nuts

1 teaspoon ground cinnamon

½ cup butter, melted

1 In large bowl, mix 2 cups of the flour, ⅓ cup sugar, the salt and yeast. In 1-quart saucepan, heat water and ⅓ cup butter over medium-low heat, stirring frequently, until very warm (120°F to 130°F). Add water mixture and egg to flour mixture. Beat with whisk or electric mixer on low speed 1 minute, until smooth. Beat on medium speed 1 minute. Stir in enough of the remaining flour, ½ cup at a time, until dough is soft, leaves side of bowl and is easy to handle (dough may be slightly sticky).

2 Place dough on lightly floured surface; turn to coat with flour. Knead dough about 10 minutes, until dough is smooth and springy. Spray large bowl with cooking spray. Place dough in bowl, turning dough to grease all sides. Cover bowl loosely with plastic wrap; let rise in warm place 1 hour to 1 hour 30 minutes or until dough has doubled in size. Dough is ready if indentation remains when touched.

3 Spray 10-inch angel food (tube) cake pan or 12-cup fluted tube cake pan with baking spray with flour (if 10-inch angel food pan has removable bottom, line pan with foil before spraying to help prevent sugar mixture from dripping in oven during baking). In small bowl, mix ¾ cup sugar, the nuts and cinnamon.

4 Gently push fist into dough to deflate. Shape dough into about 25 balls, 1½ inches in diameter. Dip each ball into melted butter, then into cinnamon-sugar. Place single layer of balls in pan so they just touch. Top with another layer of balls. Drizzle any remaining butter over balls and sprinkle with any remaining cinnamon-sugar. Cover pan loosely with plastic wrap; let rise in warm place about 40 minutes or until dough has doubled in size.

5 Meanwhile, move oven rack to low position so that top of pan will be in center of oven. Heat oven to 375°F.

Continues

Monkey Bread *continued*

6 Remove plastic wrap. Bake 35 to 40 minutes or until golden brown. (If bread browns too quickly, cover loosely with foil.) Run a metal spatula or knife around edge of pan to loosen bread. Place heatproof plate upside down over pan; turn plate and pan over together. Let stand 1 minute so butter-sugar mixture can drizzle over bread; remove pan. Serve bread while warm, pulling it apart using 2 forks or your fingers.

1 SERVING Calories 270; Total Fat 13g (Saturated Fat 6g, Trans Fat 0g); Cholesterol 40mg; Sodium 220mg; Total Carbohydrate 35g (Dietary Fiber 1g); Protein 4g **CARBOHYDRATE CHOICES:** 2

Cherry and eggnog—two flavors that have been around as long as we can remember. Pairing them together in a breakfast pastry creates a deliciousness that's hard to resist. You can get your Betty on, serving these beauties!

Cherry-Eggnog Cream Pastries

PREP TIME: 50 Minutes | START TO FINISH: 9 Hours 30 Minutes | *12 pastries*

PASTRY

4 to 5 cups all-purpose flour

⅓ cup granulated sugar

1 teaspoon salt

1 package fast-acting dry yeast (2¼ teaspoons)

1 cup milk

⅔ cup butter, cut into pieces

1 whole egg

FILLING

3 oz cream cheese (from 8-oz package), softened

1 tablespoon granulated sugar

2 egg yolks

⅛ to ¼ teaspoon rum extract

Dash ground nutmeg

1 tablespoon water

36 to 48 cherries with pie filling (from 21-oz can)

ICING

¾ cup powdered sugar

¼ teaspoon rum extract

3 to 4 teaspoons milk

1 In large bowl, stir 2 cups of the flour, the granulated sugar, salt and yeast. In 1-quart saucepan, heat 1 cup milk and the butter until very warm (120°F to 130°F). Add milk mixture and egg to flour mixture. Beat with electric mixer on low speed 1 minute. Beat on medium speed 1 minute, scraping bowl occasionally. Stir in enough of remaining flour, ½ cup at a time, to make dough easy to handle.

2 On lightly floured surface, knead dough until smooth, about 5 minutes. Cover with large bowl; let rest 10 minutes.

3 Line 2 large cookie sheets with cooking parchment paper. Divide dough into 24 equal pieces. Roll each piece into 12-inch rope. Twist 2 ropes together; coil into circle with edge built up higher than center. On cookie sheets, place pastries 3 inches apart. Cover loosely with plastic wrap sprayed with cooking spray. Let rise in warm place 45 minutes or until almost doubled in size.

4 Meanwhile, heat oven to 350°F.

5 In small bowl, stir cream cheese, granulated sugar, 1 of the egg yolks, the rum extract and nutmeg with spoon until smooth. Remove plastic wrap. Gently shape each pastry with fingers to form 2-inch-wide indentation in center. In small bowl, stir together remaining egg yolk and water; brush dough with egg yolk–water mixture. Spoon 1½ teaspoons of the cream cheese mixture into one side of each indentation; spoon 3 or 4 cherries into other side.

6 Bake 20 to 25 minutes or until golden brown. Remove from cookie sheets to cooling racks; cool 30 minutes.

7 In small bowl, mix icing ingredients until smooth and thin enough to drizzle. Drizzle icing over pastries.

Continues

Cherry-Eggnog Cream Pastries continued

1 PASTRY Calories 390; Total Fat 15g (Saturated Fat 9g, Trans Fat 0.5g); Cholesterol 80mg; Sodium 330mg; Total Carbohydrate 57g (Dietary Fiber 1g); Protein 6g **CARBOHYDRATE CHOICES:** 4

Betty's Kitchen Tips: Leftover cherry pie filling can make anything festive! Spread it on toast or atop cream cheese on your breakfast bagel, or spoon over ice cream or brownies for a special treat.

Make Ahead: Prepare dough as directed—except in Step 3, do not let rise. Refrigerate at least 8 hours or overnight. About 2 hours before serving, remove pastries from refrigerator. Let stand covered in warm place 1 hour or until almost doubled in size. Proceed with Step 4.

"Perfect to take along when dropping in on friends" was the introduction to this recipe when it first appeared in our *Betty Crocker New Picture Cook Book* (1961). We've added a vanilla glaze over the years to make it even better. This is one of the all-time favorites of our staff—we are always in awe of how good it is.

Danish Puff

PREP TIME: 20 Minutes | START TO FINISH: 1 Hour 20 Minutes | *10 servings*

PASTRY
1 cup all-purpose flour
½ cup butter, softened
2 tablespoons water

TOPPING
½ cup butter
1 cup water
1 cup all-purpose flour
1 teaspoon almond extract
3 eggs

CREAMY VANILLA GLAZE
1½ cups powdered sugar
2 tablespoons butter, softened
½ teaspoon vanilla
1 to 2 tablespoons warm water or milk
Sliced almonds, toasted, if desired

1 Heat oven to 350°F.

2 In medium bowl, place 1 cup flour. Cut in ½ cup butter using pastry blender or fork until particles are size of coarse crumbs. Sprinkle 2 tablespoons water over mixture; toss with fork until pastry forms.

3 Gather pastry into ball; divide in half. On ungreased cookie sheet, pat each half into 12×3-inch rectangle about 3 inches apart.

4 In 2-quart saucepan, heat ½ cup butter and 1 cup water to rolling boil; remove from heat. Quickly stir in 1 cup flour and almond extract. Stir vigorously over low heat about 1 minute or until mixture forms ball; remove from heat. Add eggs; beat until smooth. Spread half of topping over each rectangle.

5 Bake about 1 hour or until topping is crisp and brown. Remove from pan to cooling rack; cool completely.

6 In medium bowl, mix all glaze ingredients except almonds until smooth and spreadable. Spread over tops of pastries; sprinkle with almonds.

1 SERVING Calories 370; Total Fat 23g (Saturated Fat 14g, Trans Fat 1g); Cholesterol 110mg; Sodium 180mg; Total Carbohydrate 37g (Dietary Fiber 0g); Protein 4g **CARBOHYDRATE CHOICES:** 2½

Betty's Kitchen Tips: To toast almonds, spread in ungreased shallow pan. Bake uncovered at 350°F for 6 to 10 minutes, stirring occasionally, until light brown.

Betty's Kitchen Tips: You can serve this double-textured pastry as a bread or dessert. What an elegant addition to a brunch buffet table!

Hearty breads like this one used to be made in a coffee can, but today we recognize that it's not a good practice, since materials from the can can leach into the bread. So we've adapted this easy recipe to be made in a casserole, replicating the old-fashioned look while using safe baking practices.

No-Knead Oatmeal-Molasses Bread

PREP TIME: 15 Minutes | START TO FINISH: 2 Hours 35 Minutes | *1 loaf (16 slices)*

BREAD

- 1 cup very warm water (120°F to 130°F)
- ½ cup old-fashioned or quick-cooking oats
- ¼ cup light molasses
- 3 tablespoons shortening
- 1 egg
- 2¾ cups all-purpose flour

- 1 teaspoon salt
- 1 package regular active or fast-acting dry yeast (2¼ teaspoons)

TOPPINGS

- 1 tablespoon old-fashioned or quick-cooking oats
- ½ teaspoon coarse salt

1 Grease 1½-quart round casserole with shortening or cooking spray.

2 In large bowl, mix water, ½ cup oats, the molasses, shortening and egg until well blended. In medium bowl, mix flour, salt and yeast; add to oat mixture. Beat with electric mixer on medium speed 2 minutes, scraping bowl frequently, or until smooth.

3 Spread batter evenly in casserole (batter will be sticky; smooth and pat into shape with floured hands). Sprinkle with toppings, pressing in slightly. Cover casserole loosely with plastic wrap. Let rise at room temperature about 1 hour 30 minutes or until batter has doubled in size.

4 Meanwhile, heat oven to 375°F.

5 Remove plastic wrap. Bake 30 to 35 minutes or until golden brown and sounds hollow when tapped. (If loaf browns too quickly, cover loosely with foil during last 15 minutes of baking.) Cool in casserole 5 minutes on cooling rack. Remove from casserole; let cool on cooling rack, rounded side up. Serve warm or cool.

1 SLICE Calories 130; Total Fat 3g (Saturated Fat 1g, Trans Fat 0g); Cholesterol 10mg; Sodium 230mg; Total Carbohydrate 23g (Dietary Fiber 1g); Protein 3g **CARBOHYDRATE CHOICES:** 1½

Betty's Kitchen Tips: Slice this delicious bread into wedges to serve with soup or chili.

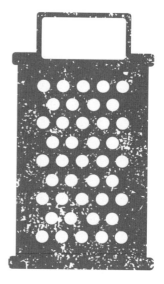

In the 1950 *Betty Crocker Picture Cookbook,* the White Bread recipe gave directions for making two or four loaves. While we aren't baking bread in those quantities any longer, even one loaf will create that irresistible aroma wafting throughout the house and the incredible taste of a warm slice slathered with butter.

Classic White Bread

PREP TIME: 35 Minutes | START TO FINISH: 3 Hours | *2 loaves (16 slices each)*

6 to 7 cups all-purpose or bread flour

3 tablespoons sugar

2 tablespoons shortening or butter, softened

1 tablespoon salt

2 packages regular active or fast-acting dry yeast (4½ teaspoons)

2¼ cups very warm water (120°F to 130°F)

2 tablespoons butter, melted, if desired

1 In large bowl, stir 3½ cups of the flour, the sugar, shortening, salt and yeast until well mixed. Add warm water; beat with electric mixer on low speed 1 minute, scraping bowl frequently. Beat on medium speed 1 minute, scraping bowl frequently. Stir in enough remaining flour, 1 cup at a time, to make dough easy to handle.

2 Place dough on lightly floured surface. Knead about 10 minutes or until dough is smooth and springy. Grease large bowl with shortening or cooking spray. Place dough in bowl, turning dough to coat all sides. Cover bowl loosely with plastic wrap; let rise in warm place 40 to 60 minutes or until dough has doubled in size. Dough is ready if indentation remains when touched.

3 Grease bottoms and sides of 2 (8×4- or 9×5-inch) loaf pans with shortening or cooking spray. Gently push fist into dough to deflate. Divide dough in half. On lightly floured surface, flatten each half with hands or rolling pin into 18×9-inch rectangle. Roll dough up tightly, beginning at 9-inch side. Press with thumbs to seal after each turn. Pinch edge of dough into roll to seal. Pinch each end of roll to seal; fold ends under loaf. Place loaves seam side down in pans. Brush loaves lightly with 1 tablespoon of the melted butter. Cover pans loosely with plastic wrap; let rise in warm place 35 to 50 minutes or until dough has doubled in size.

4 Meanwhile, move oven rack to low position so that tops of pans will be in center of oven. Heat oven to 425°F.

5 Remove plastic wrap. Bake 25 to 30 minutes or until loaves are deep golden brown and sound hollow when tapped. Remove from pans to cooling rack. Brush tops of loaves with remaining 1 tablespoon melted butter. Cool completely before slicing.

1 SLICE Calories 100; Total Fat 2g (Saturated Fat 0.5g, Trans Fat 0g); Cholesterol 0mg; Sodium 230mg; Total Carbohydrate 19g (Dietary Fiber 1g); Protein 2g **CARBOHYDRATE CHOICES: 1**

RECIPE
#27

Classic French Bread

PREP TIME: 15 Minutes | **START TO FINISH:** 3 Hours 5 Minutes | *2 loaves (12 slices each)*

3 to 3½ cups all-purpose flour or bread flour

1 tablespoon sugar

1½ teaspoons salt

1 package regular or fast-acting dry yeast (2¼ teaspoons)

1 cup very warm water (120°F to 130°F)

2 tablespoons vegetable oil

Cornmeal

1 egg white

1 tablespoon cold water

1 In large bowl, mix 2 cups of the flour, the sugar, salt and yeast. Add warm water and oil. Beat with electric mixer on low speed 1 minute, scraping bowl frequently. Beat on medium speed 1 minute, scraping bowl frequently. Stir in enough remaining flour, ½ cup at a time, to make dough easy to handle (dough will be soft).

2 On lightly floured surface, knead dough about 5 minutes or until smooth and elastic. Grease large bowl with shortening or spray with cooking spray. Place dough in bowl, turning dough to grease all sides. Cover bowl loosely with plastic wrap; let rise in warm place 1 hour 30 minutes to 2 hours or until dough has doubled in size. Dough is ready if indentation remains when touched.

3 Grease large cookie sheet with shortening or cooking spray; sprinkle with cornmeal. Gently push fist into dough to deflate. Turn dough onto lightly floured surface; divide in half. Roll each half into 15×8-inch rectangle. Roll dough up tightly, beginning at 15-inch side, to form a loaf. Pinch edge of dough into roll to seal. Pinch ends under to seal; shape ends to taper. Place both loaves seam side down on cookie sheet. Cut ¼-inch-deep slashes across tops of loaves at 2-inch intervals with sharp or serrated knife. Cover loaves loosely with plastic wrap sprayed with cooking spray. Let rise in warm place about 1 hour or until dough has doubled in size.

4 Meanwhile, place 8- or 9-inch square pan on bottom oven rack; add hot water to pan until about ½ inch from top. Heat oven to 375°F.

5 Remove plastic wrap. In small bowl, mix egg white and 1 tablespoon cold water; brush over loaves.

6 Bake 18 to 20 minutes or until loaves are golden brown and sound hollow when tapped. Remove from cookie sheet to cooling rack. Serve warm or cool.

1 SLICE Calories 70; Total Fat 1.5g (Saturated Fat 0g, Trans Fat 0g); Cholesterol 0mg; Sodium 150mg; Total Carbohydrate 13g (Dietary Fiber 0g); Protein 2g **CARBOHYDRATE CHOICES:** 1

SEEDED FRENCH BREAD: Prepare as directed—except sprinkle loaves with poppy seed and/or sesame seed after brushing with egg white and water.

PESTO-PARMESAN FRENCH BREAD: Prepare as directed—except add ¼ cup prepared pesto with water in Step 1. After dough is beaten on medium speed, stir in ¼ cup grated Parmesan cheese and enough remaining flour to make dough easy to handle. Continue as directed.

Continues

Classic French Bread continued

WHOLE WHEAT FRENCH BREAD: Prepare as directed—except use 1½ cups whole wheat flour and 1½ cups all-purpose flour. Substitute maple syrup for sugar.

BREAD MACHINE FRENCH BREAD: Place 3½ cups flour, the sugar, salt, yeast, water and oil in bread machine pan in the order recommended by the manufacturer. Select Dough/Manual cycle. Do not use delay cycle. Remove dough from pan to lightly floured surface using lightly floured hands. Cover; let rest 10 minutes. Continue as directed in Step 3.

CRUSTY HARD ROLLS: Prepare as directed—except grease large cookie sheet with shortening or cooking spray; sprinkle with cornmeal. After deflating dough, divide into 12 equal parts. Shape each part into a ball; place on cookie sheet. Brush rolls with cold water. Let rise uncovered about 1 hour or until dough has doubled in size. Heat oven to 425°F. In small bowl, mix egg white and cold water; brush over rolls. Sprinkle with poppy seed or sesame seed. Bake 15 to 20 minutes or until brown.

Betty's Kitchen Tips: To get a classic French bread crust, use a small amount of cornmeal on the cookie sheet to lift dough slightly off pan, so that air can get underneath and bake bread with golden brown crisp bottom crust. Also, placing a pan of hot water in your oven helps replicate what commercial ovens do with steam to get a nice crust.

The Betty Crocker Kitchens— Then and Now

In the beginning, new recipes and home appliances were tested in the Betty Crocker kitchens by staff home economists. Betty shared her wisdom about all things related to the management of the home, from how to iron everything from underwear to swirling skirts with petticoats to tips for spring cleaning—and how to keep your husband happy while doing them! Letters from consumers were also answered by the home economists as "Betty Crocker"—as many as 5,000 letters per week.

Today, recipe developers with backgrounds in food science, dietetics or with culinary degrees develop recipes for websites, cookbooks and social media, using the most popular appliances people have in their own kitchens. Everything is scrutinized to be sure the recipes can be made successfully—from making sure every ingredient is accounted for in the recipe, to the proper size bowls or pans being used and the temperature and time given for every step. The recipes are prepared again by a check tester and then copyedited. And what about the letters? The Consumer Relations department now answers over a million letters, emails and social media posts every year.

Our Italian Breadstick recipe in the 1964 *Betty Crocker New Picture Cookbook* instructed bakers to make pencil-thin breadsticks. Trending today are thick, chewy breadsticks, brushed with garlic butter, that you can really sink your teeth into, so we've updated this recipe. Yum!

Italian Breadsticks

PREP TIME: 35 Minutes | **START TO FINISH:** 2 Hours 10 Minutes | *12 breadsticks*

- 2 to 2¼ cups all-purpose or bread flour
- 1 tablespoon sugar
- 1 teaspoon salt
- 1 package regular or fast-acting dry yeast (2¼ teaspoons)
- ⅔ cup very warm water (120°F to 130°F)
- ¼ cup olive or vegetable oil
- 2 tablespoons butter, melted
- ½ teaspoon garlic powder

1 Grease large cookie sheet with shortening or cooking spray. In large bowl, mix 1 cup of the flour, the sugar, salt and yeast. Add water and oil; beat with electric mixer on low speed 1 minute, scraping bowl frequently. Stir in enough remaining flour, ½ cup at a time, until dough is soft and easy to handle (dough may be slightly sticky).

2 Place dough on lightly floured work surface. Knead about 5 minutes or until dough is smooth and springy. Divide dough into 12 pieces; shape and roll each piece into 6-inch-long breadstick. On cookie sheet, place breadsticks 1 inch apart. Cover breadsticks loosely with plastic wrap sprayed with cooking spray. Let rise in warm place 30 minutes or until doubled in size.

3 Meanwhile, heat oven to 350°F.

4 Remove plastic wrap. Bake 25 to 30 minutes or until golden brown. In small bowl, stir butter and garlic powder until well mixed. Brush onto breadsticks. Remove from cookie sheet to cooling rack. Serve warm or cool.

1 BREADSTICK Calories 140; Total Fat 7g (Saturated Fat 2g, Trans Fat 0g); Cholesterol 5mg; Sodium 210mg; Total Carbohydrate 17g (Dietary Fiber 0g); Protein 2g **CARBOHYDRATE CHOICES:** 1

SEEDED OR SALTY BREAD STICKS: Prepare as directed—except omit garlic powder. Before baking, brush breadsticks with butter; sprinkle with everything bagel seasoning, poppy seed, sesame seed or coarse salt.

Seeded and Salty
Breadsticks

Our Consumer Relations team answers more than 1 million requests for recipes and questions about our products each year. We've gotten lots of requests for multigrain loaves baked traditionally or with a bread machine. So we took our favorite multigrain recipe and are giving you both ways to make it!

Multigrain Bread

PREP TIME: 25 Minutes | START TO FINISH: 2 Hours 55 Minutes | *1 loaf (16 slices)*

1½ cups all-purpose flour or bread flour

3 tablespoons packed brown sugar

3 tablespoons vegetable oil

1½ teaspoons salt

1 package regular active or fast-acting dry yeast (2¼ teaspoons)

1 cup very warm water (120°F to 130°F)

1½ cups ready-to-eat 7-grain cereal

½ cup raw sunflower nuts

1 to 1½ cups whole wheat flour

1 In large bowl, mix all-purpose flour, brown sugar, 2 tablespoons of the oil, the salt and yeast. Add warm water; beat with electric mixer on low speed 1 minute, scraping bowl frequently. Beat on medium speed 1 minute, scraping bowl frequently. Stir in cereal and sunflower nuts. Stir in enough whole wheat flour, ½ cup at a time, to make dough easy to handle.

2 Turn dough onto lightly floured surface. Knead about 10 minutes or until smooth and elastic. Spray large bowl with cooking spray. Place dough in bowl, turning dough to grease all sides. Cover; let rise in warm place about 1 hour or until doubled in size. Dough is ready if indentation remains when touched.

3 Grease bottom and sides of 8×4- or 9×5-inch loaf pan with shortening or cooking spray.

4 Gently push fist into dough to deflate. On lightly floured surface, flatten dough with hands or rolling pin into rectangle 18×9 inches. Roll up tightly, beginning at 9-inch side. Press with thumbs to seal after each turn. Pinch edge of dough into roll to seal. Press each end with side of hand to seal; fold ends under loaf. Place seam side down in pan. Brush loaf lightly with remaining 1 tablespoon oil. Cover pan loosely with plastic wrap; let rise in warm place 45 minutes to 1 hour or until doubled in size.

5 Meanwhile, move oven rack to low position so that top of pan will be in center of oven. Heat oven to 400°F.

6 Remove plastic wrap. Bake 25 to 30 minutes or until loaf is deep golden brown and sounds hollow when tapped. Remove from pan to wire rack; cool before slicing.

1 SLICE Calories 150; Total Fat 5g (Saturated Fat 0.5g, Trans Fat 0g); Cholesterol 0mg; Sodium 240mg; Total Carbohydrate 22g (Dietary Fiber 1g); Protein 3g **CARBOHYDRATE CHOICES:** 1½

BREAD MACHINE SUNFLOWER SEVEN-GRAIN BREAD: For 2-pound loaf, measure ingredients into bread machine pan in the order recommended by the manufacturer. Increase water to 1½ cups; substitute softened butter for 2 tablespoons oil; use bread flour; use 1½ cups whole wheat flour; decrease cereal to 1¼ cups; increase brown sugar to ¼ cup; substitute 2½ teaspoons bread machine yeast. Omit third tablespoon oil. Select Basic/White cycle.

Betty's Kitchen Tips: We've cleverly used ready-to-eat 7-grain cereal to eliminate the need to buy 7 different grains to make this wholesome bread.

Created for *Betty Crocker Right-Size Recipes, Delicious Recipes for One or Two* (2019), we love this heavenly scented loaf that's just the right size for smaller households.

RECIPE

#30

Small-Batch No-Knead Rosemary-Parmesan Bread

PREP TIME: 20 Minutes | START TO FINISH: 2 Hours 10 Minutes | *4 servings*

- 1 to 1¼ cups all-purpose flour
- ¾ teaspoon sugar
- ½ teaspoon regular active dry yeast
- ¼ teaspoon salt
- 6 tablespoons warm water (105°F to 115°F)
- 6 teaspoons olive oil
- 3 tablespoons grated Parmesan cheese
- 3 teaspoons chopped fresh rosemary leaves
- 2 teaspoons finely chopped garlic

1 In large bowl, mix ½ cup of the flour, the sugar, yeast and salt. Stir in water and 4½ teaspoons of the oil until well mixed. Beat 2 minutes with wooden spoon.

2 Stir in ½ cup of the remaining flour, 2 tablespoons of the Parmesan cheese, 2 teaspoons of the rosemary and the garlic.

3 Stir in additional flour, 1 tablespoon at a time, until dough leaves side of bowl, flour is mixed in and dough is not sticky. Cover with plastic wrap; let rise in warm place until doubled in size, about 1 hour.

4 Line cookie sheet with cooking parchment paper. With floured hands, shape dough into 5-inch round; place on cookie sheet. Cover loosely with plastic wrap sprayed with cooking spray. Let rise in warm place about 30 to 45 minutes or until dough almost doubles in size.

5 Meanwhile, heat oven to 400°F.

6 Remove plastic wrap. Carefully brush top of loaf with ½ teaspoon of the remaining oil. Bake 15 minutes. Remove from oven. Brush loaf with another ½ teaspoon oil. Sprinkle top of loaf with remaining 1 tablespoon Parmesan cheese and 1 teaspoon rosemary; drizzle remaining ½ teaspoon oil over rosemary. Return to oven; bake 5 to 8 minutes longer or until golden brown. Serve warm, cut in wedges.

1 SERVING Calories 200; Total Fat 8g (Saturated Fat 2g, Trans Fat 0g); Cholesterol 0mg; Sodium 220mg; Total Carbohydrate 26g (Dietary Fiber 1g); Protein 5g **CARBOHYDRATE CHOICES:** 2

Betty's Kitchen Tips: You can tell your dough has risen by using your finger to make a small dent in the dough in the top of the loaf. If the dent remains, the bread is ready to bake.

Betty's Kitchen Tips: Serve this delicious bread with olive oil mixed with chopped fresh or dried herbs to dip it in. Yum!

RECIPE

#31

Pretzel rolls always seem to be the first rolls to disappear from a potluck. From the *Betty Crocker Christmas Cookbook* (2017), these soft pretzel rolls are amazing, whether at a special holiday meal or a summer get-together.

Soft Pretzel Rolls

PREP TIME: 45 Minutes | START TO FINISH: 2 Hours 45 Minutes | *18 rolls*

ROLLS

3½ to 4½ cups all-purpose flour

½ cup whole wheat flour

2 tablespoons packed brown sugar

¾ teaspoon table salt

1 package fast-acting dry yeast (2¼ teaspoons)

1½ cups very warm water (120°F to 130°F)

SODA BATH

2 quarts water

¼ cup baking soda

1 tablespoon packed brown sugar

TOPPING

1 egg yolk

1 tablespoon water

2 teaspoons coarse (kosher or sea) salt

1 In large bowl, mix 2 cups of the all-purpose flour, the whole wheat flour, brown sugar, table salt and yeast. Add warm water; beat with electric mixer on low speed 1 minute, scraping bowl occasionally. Beat on medium speed 1 minute, scraping bowl frequently. With spoon, stir in enough of the remaining all-purpose flour, ½ cup at a time, until dough is soft and leaves side of bowl.

2 On lightly floured surface, knead dough 5 minutes or until smooth and elastic. Spray large bowl with cooking spray. Place dough in bowl, turning dough to grease all sides. Cover bowl loosely with plastic wrap and cloth towel; let rise in warm place 1 hour or until doubled in size.

3 Line 2 large cookie sheets with cooking parchment paper; spray with cooking spray. Divide dough into 18 equal pieces; shape into rolls. On cookie sheets, place rolls 3 inches apart. Cover rolls loosely with plastic wrap; let rise 30 to 45 minutes or until almost doubled in size.

4 Heat oven to 425°F. In large stockpot, heat 2 quarts water to boiling. Stir in baking soda and 1 tablespoon brown sugar until dissolved (mixture will foam). Reduce heat to low. Carefully place 3 rolls in simmering water. Cook 30 seconds; turn and cook 30 seconds longer. With slotted spoon, remove rolls and return to cookie sheet. Repeat with remaining rolls.

5 In small bowl, beat egg yolk and water. Brush egg mixture over each roll. Using scissors or serrated knife, cut ½-inch crosses in center of each roll. Sprinkle with coarse salt.

6 Bake 10 to 15 minutes or until deep golden brown. Remove from cookie sheets to cooling racks. Serve warm or at room temperature.

1 ROLL Calories 110; Total Fat 0.5g (Saturated Fat 0g, Trans Fat 0g); Cholesterol 10mg; Sodium 430mg; Total Carbohydrate 23g (Dietary Fiber 1g); Protein 3g **CARBOHYDRATE CHOICES:** 1½

Make Ahead: Rolls can be made through Step 3 a day before baking. Once they're placed on the cookie sheets, cover with plastic wrap and refrigerate overnight. Remove rolls from refrigerator and let stand at room temperate 30 minutes or until almost doubled. Continue as directed in Step 4.

"The memory of a cozy kitchen filled with the warm fragrance of freshly baked bread still means home." Written in the yeast breads chapter opener in our 1950 cookbook, this is still true—nothing's changed today! Originally a loaf bread with the addition of ½ teaspoon ground nutmeg, we've given this recipe a makeover, with today's yeast, in an easy bun recipe.

No-Knead Herb Buns

PREP TIME: 25 Minutes | **START TO FINISH:** 3 Hours 20 Minutes | *12 buns*

2¼ cups all-purpose flour
2 tablespoons sugar
1 teaspoon caraway seed
½ teaspoon dried sage leaves
½ teaspoon salt
1 package regular active or fast-acting dry yeast (2¼ teaspoons)

1 cup very warm water (120°F to 130°F)
2 tablespoons shortening or butter, softened
1 egg

1 Grease 12 regular-size muffin cups with shortening or cooking spray.

2 In large bowl, mix 1 cup of the flour, the sugar, caraway seed, sage, salt and yeast. Add water, shortening and egg; beat with electric mixer on high speed 2 minutes, scraping bowl frequently. Stir in the remaining flour until soft, sticky dough forms. Cover bowl loosely with plastic wrap; let rise 1 hour or until dough has doubled in size.

3 Spoon about ¼ cup dough into each muffin cup. Cover buns loosely with plastic wrap sprayed with cooking spray; let rise 1 hour or until dough reaches tops of cups.

4 Meanwhile, heat oven to 400°F.

5 Remove plastic wrap. Bake 12 to 15 minutes or until golden brown. Remove from muffin cups to cooling rack. Serve warm.

1 BUN Calories 120; Total Fat 3g (Saturated Fat 0.5g, Trans Fat 0g); Cholesterol 15mg; Sodium 105mg; Total Carbohydrate 20g (Dietary Fiber 1g); Protein 3g **CARBOHYDRATE CHOICES:** 1

Make Ahead: For fresh, hot buns in a few minutes, simply bake and cool buns ahead of time. Wrap desired quantities in foil and place in a resealable freezer plastic bag. Freeze up to 3 months. Heat foil-wrapped buns in a 350°F oven about 30 minutes. They will taste like you just made them fresh!

Debuting in the 1956 *Betty Crocker Picture Cookbook,* this recipe has survived basically untouched, except for being updated for today's yeast and substituting softened butter for the shortening for added flavor. It's a super way to have hot, fresh rolls whenever you like!

Make-Ahead Potato Roll Dough

PREP TIME: 30 Minutes | START TO FINISH: 9 Hours 45 Minutes | *32 to 64 rolls*

- 7 to 7½ cups all-purpose flour
- ⅔ cup sugar
- 1½ teaspoons salt
- 1 package regular active dry yeast (2¼ teaspoons)
- 1½ cups very warm water (120°F to 130°F)

- 1 cup lukewarm unseasoned mashed potatoes (about 1 large potato; no butter or cream)
- ⅔ cup butter, softened
- 2 eggs

1 In large bowl, mix 3 cups of the flour, the sugar, salt and yeast. Add water, potatoes, butter and eggs. Beat with electric mixer on low speed 1 minute, scraping bowl frequently. Beat on medium speed 1 minute, scraping bowl frequently. Stir in enough remaining flour, ½ cup at a time, to make dough easy to handle.

2 Place dough on lightly floured surface. Knead 5 minutes or until dough is smooth and springy. Spray large bowl with cooking spray. Place dough in bowl, turning dough to grease all sides. Cover bowl tightly with plastic wrap and refrigerate at least 8 hours but no longer than 5 days.

3 Divide dough into 4 equal pieces. Use one-fourth of the dough for any roll recipe below.

1 CRESCENT ROLL Calories 80; Total Fat 2.5g (Saturated Fat 1.5g, Trans Fat 0g); Cholesterol 10mg; Sodium 80mg; Total Carbohydrate 13g (Dietary Fiber 0g); Protein 1g **CARBOHYDRATE CHOICES:** 1

CRESCENT ROLLS: Grease cookie sheet with shortening or cooking spray. Roll one-fourth of potato roll dough into 12-inch circle about ¼-inch thick on well-floured surface. Spread with 2 tablespoons softened butter. Cut circle into 16 wedges. Roll up each wedge, beginning at rounded edge, stretching dough as it is rolled. On cookie sheet, place rolls about 2 inches apart, with points underneath; curve slightly. Brush with melted butter, if desired. Cover with plastic wrap; let stand in warm place about 1 hour or until doubled in size. Heat oven to 400°F. Bake 10 to 13 minutes or until golden brown. 16 crescent rolls.

FLOWER ROLLS: Grease bottoms and sides of 8 to 10 regular-size muffin cups with shortening or cooking spray. Shape one-fourth of potato roll dough into 8 to 10 (2-inch) balls. Place 1 ball in each muffin cup. With kitchen scissors, snip each ball into fourths, cutting completely through balls. Brush with 1 tablespoon melted butter. Cover with plastic wrap; let stand in warm place 1 hour. Heat oven to 400°F. Bake 14 to 16 minutes or until golden brown. 8 to 10 flower rolls.

DINNER ROLLS: Grease 12 regular-size muffin cups. Shape one-fourth of potato roll dough into 12 balls. Place 1 ball in each muffin cup. Brush with 1 tablespoon melted butter; sprinkle with coarse salt. Let rise, and bake as directed for Flower Rolls. 12 rolls.

Continues

Crescent, Flower and
Dinner Rolls

Make-Ahead Potato Roll Dough *continued*

MAKE-AHEAD WHOLE WHEAT–POTATO ROLL DOUGH: Prepare as directed—except substitute 3 to 4 cups whole wheat flour for second addition of all-purpose flour.

MAKE-AHEAD BROWN-AND-SERVE ROLLS: Shape potato roll dough for Crescent Rolls or Flower Rolls as directed above. Cover; let rise in warm place about 1 hour. Heat oven to 275°F. Bake 20 minutes (do not allow to brown). Remove from pan; cool to room temperature. Wrap in foil. Store in refrigerator up to 8 days or in freezer up to 2 months. At serving time, heat oven to 400°F. Bake 8 to 12 minutes or until brown.

Our Consumer Relations department tells us that many of our consumers are requesting gluten-free bread recipes. This is like an extra-credit project from the Betty Crocker Kitchens!

Gluten-Free Bagels

PREP TIME: 20 Minutes | START TO FINISH: 1 Hour 40 Minutes | *8 bagels*

1 cup very warm water (120°F to 130°F)

1 package regular active dry yeast (2¼ teaspoons)

4 teaspoons sugar

2¼ cups Betty Crocker Gluten Free all-purpose rice flour blend

1 tablespoon gluten-free baking powder

1½ teaspoons baking soda

1 teaspoon xanthan gum

½ teaspoon salt

1 egg

½ teaspoon cider vinegar

2 quarts water

1 egg white

1 tablespoon water

1 tablespoon sesame seed

1 Line large cookie sheet with cooking parchment paper; spray with cooking spray (without flour). In small bowl, stir together 1 cup water, the yeast and 3 teaspoons of the sugar until dissolved. Set aside.

2 In large bowl, mix rice flour blend, baking powder, ½ teaspoon of the baking soda, the xanthan gum and salt. Stir in yeast mixture, egg and vinegar until well blended (dough will be soft and slightly sticky). Divide dough into 8 pieces; shape into balls. Using your finger, form 1-inch diameter hole in center of each ball, to look like bagel. On cookie sheet, place bagels 2 inches apart. Cover with plastic wrap; let rise in warm place 45 minutes (dough won't double in size).

3 Heat oven to 375°F. Meanwhile, in 4-quart saucepan, heat 2 quarts water, the remaining 1 teaspoon sugar and 1 teaspoon baking soda to boiling over medium-high heat. Gently add 2 bagels at a time to water; simmer 1 minute. Using slotted spoon, turn bagels over; simmer 1 minute longer. Return to cookie sheet. Repeat with remaining bagels.

4 In small bowl, beat egg white and 1 tablespoon water; brush tops of bagels. Sprinkle with sesame seed.

5 Bake 20 to 25 minutes or until golden brown. Remove from cookie sheet to cooling rack. Serve warm or cool.

Continues

Everything Bagels

Gluten-Free Bagels *continued*

1 BAGEL Calories 150; Total Fat 1.5g (Saturated Fat 0g, Trans Fat 0g); Cholesterol 25mg; Sodium 740mg; Total Carbohydrate 32g (Dietary Fiber 1g); Protein 3g **CARBOHYDRATE CHOICES:** 2

EVERYTHING BAGELS: Prepare as directed— except in small bowl, stir 2 teaspoons dried onion flakes, 1 teaspoon each poppy seed and sesame seed, ¼ teaspoon garlic powder and ¼ teaspoon kosher salt. Sprinkle on tops of bagels as directed in Step 4.

Cooking Gluten Free? Always read labels to make sure *each* recipe ingredient is gluten free. Products and ingredient sources can change.

Celebrated
Main Dishes

A recipe top rated by our Betty fans, with good reason. With only 15 minutes prep, you can pop this family favorite into the oven and be devouring the enchiladas faster than you can get takeout.

Gluten-Free Creamy Chicken Enchiladas

PREP TIME: 15 Minutes | START TO FINISH: 55 Minutes | *4 servings (2 enchiladas each)*

- 1 can (18 oz) ready-to-serve creamy mushroom soup
- 1 can (4.5 oz) chopped green chiles
- 2 teaspoons chili powder
- 1 teaspoon ground cumin
- ½ teaspoon garlic powder
- 3 cups gluten-free shredded cubed or non-basted chicken
- 2 cups gluten-free shredded Mexican cheese blend or cheddar cheese (8 oz)

- ½ cup gluten-free sour cream
- 8 (6-inch) gluten-free corn tortillas

GARNISHES, IF DESIRED

Shredded lettuce

Chopped tomatoes or salsa

Sliced green onions

Additional gluten-free sour cream

1 Heat oven to 350°F. Spray bottom of 13×9-inch (3-quart) glass baking dish with cooking spray (without flour).

2 In small bowl, mix soup, chiles, chili powder, cumin and garlic powder. Spread ½ cup of soup mixture in bottom of baking dish. In medium bowl, stir together chicken, 1 cup of the cheese, the sour cream and ½ cup of the soup mixture.

3 To soften tortillas, place 2 to 4 tortillas between dampened microwavable paper towels or microwavable plastic wrap and microwave on High 15 to 20 seconds until softened. Spoon about ⅓ cup chicken mixture down center of each tortilla. Roll up tortillas; arrange seam side down in baking dish. Repeat with remaining tortillas and chicken mixture. Top enchiladas with remaining soup mixture, completely covering them to help prevent drying and cracking. Sprinkle with remaining 1 cup cheese. Spray sheet of foil with cooking spray (without flour); cover baking dish with foil, sprayed side down.

4 Bake 30 minutes. Remove foil; bake 5 to 10 minutes longer or until hot. Top each serving with lettuce, tomatoes, onions and sour cream.

1 SERVING Calories 660; Total Fat 38g (Saturated Fat 17g, Trans Fat 1g); Cholesterol 165mg; Sodium 1340mg; Total Carbohydrate 33g (Dietary Fiber 4g); Protein 47g **CARBOHYDRATE CHOICES:** 2

Cooking Gluten Free? Always read labels to make sure *each* recipe ingredient is gluten free. Products and ingredient sources can change.

Our first stuffed pepper recipe said to "place peppers in a kettle, . . . fill with desired filling" and "bake in mod. oven." The Classic recipe variation below is a best-loved recipe on bettycrocker.com. We love this trendy take on the recipe, using a spicy Buffalo chicken filling, for a contemporary twist.

Buffalo Chicken and Jalapeño-Stuffed Peppers

PREP TIME: 20 Minutes | START TO FINISH: 1 Hour 15 Minutes | *4 servings (2 pepper halves each)*

4 large bell peppers, any color

BUFFALO CHICKEN FILLING

4 oz cream cheese (half of 8-oz package), cubed

4 tablespoons Buffalo wing sauce

¼ teaspoon garlic powder

3 cups chopped cooked chicken

2 stalks celery, diced (1 cup)

12 medium green onions, thinly sliced (¾ cup)

1 small jalapeño chile, seeded, chopped

1⅓ cups shredded mozzarella cheese

¼ cup crumbled blue cheese

1 Heat oven to 425°F. Line 18×13-inch rimmed sheet pan with cooking parchment paper. Cut each bell pepper in half lengthwise. Remove seeds and membranes; place peppers cut side up on sheet pan.

2 In large microwavable bowl, mix cream cheese, 3 tablespoons of the wing sauce and the garlic powder. Microwave on High 45 to 60 seconds until smooth, stirring every 15 seconds. Stir in chicken, celery, onions, jalapeño and 1 cup of the mozzarella cheese.

3 Divide mixture evenly among peppers (peppers will be full). Spray sheet of foil with cooking spray; cover pan with foil, sprayed side down.

4 Bake 45 minutes. Uncover; top with remaining ⅓ cup mozzarella cheese. Bake 5 to 10 minutes longer, until cheese is melted and peppers are

crisp-tender when pierced with fork. Let stand 5 minutes before serving.

5 Just before serving, drizzle with remaining 1 tablespoon wing sauce. Top peppers with blue cheese.

1 SERVING Calories 540; Total Fat 32g (Saturated Fat 15g, Trans Fat 1.5g); Cholesterol 150mg; Sodium 1090mg; Total Carbohydrate 19g (Dietary Fiber 5g); Protein 44g **CARBOHYDRATE CHOICES:** 1

CLASSIC STUFFED PEPPERS: Prepare as directed—except omit Buffalo chicken filling. Cook 1 pound ground beef with 2 tablespoons chopped onion; drain. Stir in 1 cup cooked rice, 1 teaspoon salt, 1 finely chopped clove garlic, and 1 can (15 oz) tomato sauce. Proceed with Step 3. In Step 4, substitute ¾ cup shredded mozzarella cheese.

Betty's Kitchen Tips: If your peppers won't sit straight when cut in half, slice a very thin slice from the bottom side, so that they can be filled and baked without tipping over.

Betty's Kitchen Tips: Jalapeño chiles vary in size and heat. Adjust amount based on your heat preference.

RECIPE

#37

Seasoned Oven-Roasted Chicken

PREP TIME: 10 Minutes | **START TO FINISH:** 1 Hour | *8 breasts (about 4 cups cut-up chicken)*

- 8 boneless skinless chicken breasts (about 2 lb)
- 1 tablespoon olive or vegetable oil
- 1½ teaspoons parsley flakes
- 1 teaspoon seasoned salt
- 1 teaspoon garlic-pepper blend
- 1 teaspoon dried basil leaves

1 BREAST OR ½ CUP Calories 150; Total Fat 5g (Saturated Fat 1.5g, Trans Fat 0g); Cholesterol 70mg; Sodium 240mg; Total Carbohydrate 0g (Dietary Fiber 0g); Protein 25g **CARBOHYDRATE CHOICES:** 0

Betty's Kitchen Tips: This is a great recipe to use when a recipe calls for cooked chicken. Cool cooked chicken 10 to 15 minutes. Cut into desired size pieces. Wrap tightly and refrigerate up to 2 days or place in resealable freezer plastic bags and freeze up to 1 month.

1 Heat oven to 400°F. Spray 13×9-inch (3-quart) glass baking dish with cooking spray.

2 Brush both sides of chicken with oil. Sprinkle both sides with parsley, seasoned salt, garlic-pepper blend and basil. Place in baking dish.

3 Bake uncovered 25 to 35 minutes or until juice of chicken is clear when center of thickest part is cut (instant-read meat thermometer reads at least 165°F).

This quintessential comfort food has been gracing tables for years, and it remains a favorite of our fans.

Gluten-Free Chicken and Dumplings

PREP TIME: 20 Minutes | START TO FINISH: 45 Minutes | *4 servings*

CHICKEN
- 2½ cups chicken broth
- 1½ cups cut-up cooked chicken
- 1 cup frozen mixed vegetables
- 1 teaspoon gluten-free seasoned salt
- ¼ teaspoon pepper
- 1 cup milk
- 3 tablespoons cornstarch

DUMPLINGS
- ¾ cup Bisquick Gluten Free mix
- ⅓ cup milk
- 2 tablespoons butter, melted
- 1 tablespoon chopped fresh parsley
- 1 egg

1 In 3-quart saucepan, heat broth, chicken, vegetables, salt, and pepper to boiling. In small bowl, mix 1 cup milk and the cornstarch with whisk until smooth. Stir cornstarch mixture into chicken mixture; heat just to boiling.

2 In small bowl, mix dumpling ingredients with fork until blended. Gently drop dough by 8 rounded spoonfuls onto boiling chicken mixture.

3 Cook uncovered over low heat 10 minutes. Cover; cook 15 minutes longer.

1 SERVING Calories 360; Total Fat 14g (Saturated Fat 6g, Trans Fat 0g); Cholesterol 120mg; Sodium 1390mg; Total Carbohydrate 36g (Dietary Fiber 2g); Protein 24g **CARBOHYDRATE CHOICES:** 2½

CLASSIC CHICKEN AND DUMPLINGS: Prepare as directed—except use regular (not gluten-free) ingredients with chicken, and substitute ⅓ cup all-purpose flour for cornstarch. Heat to boiling; reduce heat. Simmer, stirring frequently, 1 minute. For dumplings, substitute 2 cups Original Bisquick mix for gluten-free Bisquick, increase milk to ⅔ cup, omit butter and increase parsley to 2 tablespoons.

Cooking Gluten Free? Always read labels to make sure *each* recipe ingredient is gluten free. Products and ingredient sources can change.

In the 1961 version of "Big Red," our Tetrazzini recipe was made with turkey and ham. While that recipe continues to be a favorite, it's been updated to use chicken, which is what we tend to have on hand, making it easy to pull together.

Chicken Tetrazzini

PREP TIME: 30 Minutes | START TO FINISH: 1 Hour | *6 servings*

- 1 package (7 oz) uncooked spaghetti, broken into thirds
- 2 cups frozen sweet peas (from 12-oz bag)
- ¼ cup butter
- 1½ cups sliced fresh mushrooms (half of 8-oz package)
- ¼ cup all-purpose flour
- ½ teaspoon salt

- ¼ teaspoon pepper
- 1 cup chicken broth
- 1 cup whipping cream
- 2 cups cubed deli rotisserie chicken (from 2- to 3-lb chicken)
- 2 tablespoons dry sherry or water
- ½ cup grated Parmesan cheese

1 SERVING Calories 530; Total Fat 29g (Saturated Fat 17g, Trans Fat 1g); Cholesterol 110mg; Sodium 600mg; Total Carbohydrate 41g (Dietary Fiber 4g); Protein 26g **CARBOHYDRATE CHOICES:** 3

Betty's Kitchen Tips: You can use Seasoned Oven-Roasted Chicken (page 103) in this recipe.

Make Ahead: Make this casserole the night before; cover and refrigerate until ready to bake. It may need to bake an additional 10 minutes to become bubbly in the center.

1 Heat oven to 350°F. Cook and drain spaghetti as directed on package, using minimum cook time and adding peas during last 3 minutes of cooking.

2 Meanwhile, in 3-quart saucepan, melt butter over low heat. Add mushrooms and cook about 5 minutes, stirring frequently, just until tender. Stir in flour, salt and pepper. Cook and stir until mixture is smooth and bubbly; remove from heat.

3 Stir in broth and whipping cream. Heat to boiling, stirring constantly. Boil and stir 1 minute. Stir in spaghetti and peas, chicken and sherry. Spoon mixture into ungreased 2-quart casserole. Sprinkle with cheese.

4 Bake uncovered about 30 minutes or until bubbly in center.

RECIPE

#40

Oven-Fried Chicken Tenders

PREP TIME: 10 Minutes | **START TO FINISH:** 30 Minutes | *4 servings*

¼ cup all-purpose flour

1 egg

1 tablespoon water

1 cup plain panko crispy bread crumbs

½ cup grated Parmesan cheese

1 package (about 1¼ lb) chicken breast tenders (not breaded)

Favorite dipping sauce, if desired

1 Heat oven to 425°F. Line cookie sheet with foil; spray with cooking spray.

2 In shallow dish, place flour. In another shallow dish, beat egg and water. In third shallow dish, mix panko bread crumbs and cheese. Coat chicken with flour; dip into egg mixture, then coat with bread crumb mixture. Place on cookie sheet.

3 Bake 15 to 20 minutes, turning once, until chicken is no longer pink in center and coating is golden brown. Serve with dipping sauce.

1 SERVING Calories 370; Total Fat 11g (Saturated Fat 4g, Trans Fat 0g); Cholesterol 145mg; Sodium 320mg; Total Carbohydrate 27g (Dietary Fiber 0g); Protein 42g **CARBOHYDRATE CHOICES:** 2

CHEDDAR-BACON CHICKEN TENDERS: Prepare as directed—except heat oven to 400°F. Omit flour and water. Reduce panko bread crumbs to ½ cup. Substitute shredded cheddar cheese for Parmesan. Add 1 (3-oz) jar or package cooked real bacon bits or pieces with cheese. Use 1 (14-oz) package boneless skinless chicken tenders; dip in egg, then bread crumb mixture.

ITALIAN CHICKEN TENDERS: Prepare as directed—except use Italian style panko crispy bread crumbs. Serve with marinara sauce for dipping.

Betty's Kitchen Tips: For extra-crispy tenders, drizzle with 2 tablespoons melted butter before baking.

Betty's Kitchen Tips: Barbecue sauce, ranch dressing and honey mustard are great dipping sauce options.

How can anyone resist fried chicken? It's been a favorite since our first Betty Crocker cookbook. The recipe is basically the same except we've updated celery salt with regular salt. We've also added buttermilk and hot-and-spicy versions.

Skillet-Fried Chicken

PREP TIME: 10 Minutes | **START TO FINISH:** 40 Minutes | *6 servings*

- ½ cup all-purpose flour
- 1 tablespoon paprika
- 1½ teaspoons salt
- ½ teaspoon pepper
- 1 cut-up whole chicken (3 to 3½ lb)

 Vegetable oil

1 In shallow dish, mix flour, paprika, salt and pepper. Coat chicken with flour mixture.

2 In 12-inch nonstick skillet, heat ¼ inch oil over medium-high heat. Add chicken, skin side down; cook about 10 minutes, turning once, or until light brown on all sides.

3 Reduce heat to low. Turn chicken skin side up. Cook uncovered about 20 minutes, without turning, until juice of chicken is clear when thickest part is cut to bone (instant-read meat thermometer reads at least 165°F).

1 SERVING Calories 290; Total Fat 16g (Saturated Fat 4g, Trans Fat 0g); Cholesterol 85mg; Sodium 670mg; Total Carbohydrate 9g (Dietary Fiber 0g); Protein 28g **CARBOHYDRATE CHOICES:** ½

BUTTERMILK FRIED CHICKEN: Prepare as directed—except before Step 1, mix 1 cup buttermilk and ½ teaspoon red pepper sauce in 1-gallon resealable food-storage plastic bag. Add chicken pieces; seal bag and turn to coat. Refrigerate 1 to 2 hours to marinate. Add 1 teaspoon dried thyme leaves and ⅛ teaspoon ground nutmeg to flour mixture and proceed with Step 1.

HOT-AND-SPICY CHICKEN: Prepare as directed—except before Step 1, mix ½ cup red pepper sauce and ½ teaspoon garlic salt in 1-gallon resealable food-storage plastic bag. Add chicken pieces; seal bag and turn to coat. Refrigerate 1 to 2 hours to marinate. Proceed with Step 1.

Betty's Kitchen Tips: Using a deep-sided skillet will help control splatters.

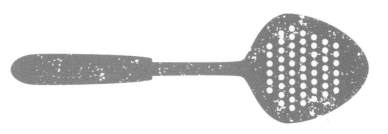

Both the Chicken Pot Pie and Impossibly Easy Chicken Pot Pie recipes rank high with our followers. We can't blame them—they're delicious and comforting. We couldn't pick between the recipes, so we included them both.

Individual Chicken Pot Pies

PREP TIME: 40 Minutes | **START TO FINISH:** 1 Hour 40 Minutes | *6 servings*

Two-Crust Pastry (page 243) or 1 box refrigerated pie crusts, softened as directed on box

⅓ cup butter

⅓ cup all-purpose flour

⅓ cup chopped onion

½ teaspoon salt

¼ teaspoon pepper

1¾ cups chicken broth

⅔ cup milk

3 cups cut-up cooked chicken or turkey

2 cups frozen peas and carrots

Additional pepper, if desired

1 Prepare pastry as directed through Step 3 of Classic Apple Pie recipe; cover with plastic wrap and set aside.

2 Lightly spray 6 (10-oz) ramekins or custard cups with cooking spray.

3 In 2-quart saucepan, melt butter over medium heat. Stir in flour, onion, salt and pepper. Cook and stir until mixture is bubbly, about 2 to 3 minutes. Stir in broth and milk. Heat to boiling, stirring constantly. Boil and stir 1 minute. Stir in chicken and peas and carrots; remove from heat.

4 Heat oven to 425°F. Using floured rolling pin, roll one round of pastry on lightly floured surface into 16-inch circle. Using one of the ramekins as a guide, cut pastry with a sharp knife at least 1 inch around the dish to make 3 pastry circles (about 5½ inches in diameter), rerolling pastry if necessary. Repeat with second pastry round to make 6 pastry circles total. Place ramekins on 15×10×1-inch baking pan. Evenly divide chicken mixture among dishes. Top each ramekin with a pastry circle, gently

pressing sides down the ramekin. Make a slit in the top of each circle.

5 Bake 30 to 35 minutes or until golden brown. Sprinkle with additional pepper.

1 SERVING Calories 570; Total Fat 32g (Saturated Fat 15g, Trans Fat 0.5g); Cholesterol 105mg; Sodium 1000mg; Total Carbohydrate 45g (Dietary Fiber 2g); Protein 26g **CARBOHYDRATE CHOICES:** 3

FAMILY-SIZE POT PIE: Prepare as directed—except roll two-thirds of pastry into 13-inch square. Ease into ungreased 9-inch square (2-quart) glass baking dish. Pour chicken mixture into pastry-lined dish. Roll remaining pastry into 11-inch square. Cut out designs with 1-inch cookie cutter. Place square over chicken mixture. Arrange cutouts on pastry. Turn both edges of pastry under; press together and flute. Bake about 35 minutes or until golden brown.

TUNA POT PIES: Prepare as directed—except substitute 1 can (12 oz) tuna in water, drained, for chicken.

IMPOSSIBLY EASY CHICKEN POT PIE: Heat oven to 400°F. Reduce chicken to 1 cup and peas and carrots to 1⅔ cups. Omit remaining ingredients. In ungreased 9-inch pie plate, mix peas and carrots, chicken, and 1 can (10¾ oz) condensed cream of chicken soup. In small bowl, mix 1 cup Original Bisquick mix, ½ cup milk and 1 egg; pour into pie plate over filling. Bake 30 minutes or until golden brown.

Continues

Individual Chicken Pot Pies continued

Betty's Kitchen Tips: Pot pies are a great way to use up leftover cooked meat, poultry, fish and/or veggies. Cut into bite-size pieces. Use 4 to 5 cups of any combination of ingredients to stir into the sauce.

Make Ahead: Make extra individual pot pies for an easy dinner later in the week. Let cool at room temperature 30 minutes after baking. Cover loosely and refrigerate up to 3 days. When ready to bake, uncover and place on a cookie sheet. Bake at 375°F for 20 to 30 minutes or until a table knife inserted in the center feels hot when touched with a finger.

Foolproof
Turkey
Gravy

grateful

Roast Turkey
with Fresh
Thyme Rub
and Maple
Glaze

Bread Stuffing

Our Best Holiday Feast

Nothing says holiday like a perfectly browned bird on the center of the table! Here are our favorite recipes for turkey, stuffing and gravy—foolproof, and so delicious your guests will be wowed and will surely want seconds. Round out the spread with your favorite side dishes and desserts or ask guests to each bring a dish. These building-block recipes are perfect for any holiday or special gathering— change up what you serve with them to fit the occasion and the season!

A Dive into Thanksgiving Sides

Did you know that what we put on the Thanksgiving table hasn't always been the same? Here's how the big meal has changed or stayed the same over the years.

Pilgrim Picks

The voyage on the *Mayflower* depleted the ship's pantry, so they ate off the land. Corn was cooked in a thick mush or porridge and sometimes sweetened with molasses. There wasn't any sugar to sweeten the cranberries, nor butter and wheat to make a pie crust. The first pumpkin pies were a custard made by roasting hollowed-out pumpkins filled with milk, honey and spices. Potatoes weren't available, but nuts and turnips were.

Continues

Fancy Fixings of the Late 1800s

Thanksgiving became a series of courses before and after the turkey. The feast might include oyster or tomato soup, followed by fish with egg sauce and either boiled or mashed potatoes, then chicken croquettes, stewed salsify (a turnip cousin) and pickles. Then came the turkey with stuffing, gravy, cranberries and sweet potatoes, followed by salad, cheese and crackers, and pumpkin pie.

Color Comes in the Mid-1900s

Stewed corn, lettuce wedges with Thousand Island dressing, gelatin salads and jellied cranberries from a can were in vogue. Green bean casserole was invented, and fruited coleslaw graced Thanksgiving tables.

Flavor Twists of Today

Familiar dishes done in new ways is now how we keep traditions but make them fresh—stuffing muffins, mashed cauliflower instead of potatoes, or twists on traditional dishes, such as creamed kale, quinoa stuffing or cranberry-pomegranate relish. Pumpkin shows up in more than just pie, from alcoholic drinks to bread and cakes.

Throughout the generations, cooks have turned to Betty Crocker for their holiday meals because they know they can count on Betty for recipes that work and that their families will love. This is a favorite because it has both a flavorful rub and a complimentary glaze. Doubly delicious!

Roast Turkey with Fresh Thyme Rub and Maple Glaze

PREP TIME: 20 Minutes | START TO FINISH: 4 Hours 20 Minutes | *12 servings*

- 1 whole turkey (12 lb), thawed if frozen
- 2 tablespoons butter
- 3 tablespoons chopped fresh thyme leaves
- 1 teaspoon salt
- ½ teaspoon ground allspice
- ½ teaspoon pepper
- 1 tablespoon olive oil
- 2 tablespoons real maple or maple-flavored syrup

1 Heat oven to 325°F. Discard giblets and neck or reserve for another use. Rinse turkey inside and out with cold water; pat dry with paper towels.

2 Fold wings across back of turkey so tips are touching. If turkey doesn't have an ovenproof plastic leg band holding legs together, tuck legs under band of skin at tail (if present) or tie legs together with kitchen string, then tie to tail if desired. Place turkey breast side up on rack in large roasting pan. Melt 1 tablespoon of the butter; brush over turkey.

3 In small bowl, mix thyme, salt, allspice, pepper and oil. Rub mixture over turkey. Insert ovenproof meat thermometer into turkey so tip is in thickest part of inside thigh and does not touch bone.

4 Roast uncovered 3 hours to 3 hours 45 minutes. After roasting about 2 hours, cut plastic band, skin or string holding legs, to allow inside of thighs to cook thoroughly and evenly. Place tent of foil loosely over turkey to prevent excessive browning.

5 Melt remaining 1 tablespoon butter; mix with syrup. Brush half of the mixture over turkey about 20 minutes before completely cooked. Brush again about 10 minutes before completely cooked.

6 Turkey is done when thermometer reads 165°F and legs move easily when lifted or twisted. Remove turkey from pan to warm platter (reserve pan drippings for gravy, page 121, if desired); cover with foil to keep warm. Let stand 15 minutes for easiest carving.

1 SERVING Calories 360; Total Fat 14g (Saturated Fat 4.5g, Trans Fat 0g); Cholesterol 230mg; Sodium 430mg; Total Carbohydrate 2g (Dietary Fiber 0g); Protein 57g **CARBOHYDRATE CHOICES:** 0

Betty Kitchen Tips: For optimal food safety and even doneness, the USDA recommends cooking stuffing separately. Cooking home-stuffed poultry or game birds is riskier than cooking those that are not stuffed. However, if you choose to stuff poultry or game birds, it's necessary to use an accurate food thermometer to make sure the center of the stuffing has reached a safe minimum temperature of 165°F. Even if the poultry or game bird itself has reached the safe minimum internal temperature of 165°F, the stuffing may not have reached the same temperature. Bacteria can survive in stuffing that has not reached 165°F, possibly resulting in food-borne illness. Do not stuff poultry or game birds that will be grilled, smoked, fried or microwaved because they will never get hot enough in the center to be safe.

What's turkey without the stuffing? This is a classic everyone will love. And there are several variations to customize it to your tastes.

Bread Stuffing

PREP TIME: **15 Minutes** | START TO FINISH: **55 Minutes** | *12 servings (½ cup each)*

¾ cup butter

2 large stalks celery (with leaves), chopped (1½ cups)

1 medium onion, chopped (1 cup)

9 cups soft bread cubes (about 15 slices bread)

1½ teaspoons chopped fresh or ½ teaspoon dried thyme leaves

1½ teaspoons chopped fresh or ½ teaspoon dried sage leaves or ¼ teaspoon ground sage

1 teaspoon salt

¼ teaspoon pepper

1 Heat oven to 350°F. Grease 13×9-inch (3-quart) glass baking dish with shortening or cooking spray.

2 In 4-quart saucepan or Dutch oven, melt butter over medium-high heat. Add celery and onion and cook 4 to 6 minutes, stirring occasionally, until tender. Add remaining ingredients; stir gently to mix well. Spoon into baking dish.

3 Cover with foil; bake 25 minutes. Remove foil; bake 10 to 15 minutes longer or until center is hot and edges are beginning to brown.

1 SERVING Calories 240; Total Fat 15g (Saturated Fat 9g, Trans Fat 0.5g); Cholesterol 35mg; Sodium 560mg; Total Carbohydrate 23g (Dietary Fiber 1g); Protein 4g **CARBOHYDRATE CHOICES:** 1½

CORNBREAD STUFFING: Prepare as directed—except substitute cornbread cubes for soft bread cubes.

CORNBREAD-SAUSAGE STUFFING: Prepare Cornbread Stuffing except omit salt; add ½ pound cooked and crumbled bulk pork or chorizo sausage (see Sausage Stuffing, right) and 1 cup chopped toasted pecans with the remaining stuffing ingredients.

GIBLET STUFFING: Prepare as directed—except place giblets and neck (but not liver) from turkey or chicken in 2-quart saucepan. Add enough water to cover; season with salt and pepper. Simmer uncovered over low heat 1 to 2 hours or until tender; drain. Remove meat from neck and finely chop with giblets; add with the remaining stuffing ingredients.

OYSTER STUFFING: Prepare as directed—except add 2 cans (8 oz each) whole oysters, drained and chopped, with the remaining stuffing ingredients.

SAUSAGE STUFFING: Prepare as directed—except omit salt. In 10-inch skillet, cook 1 pound bulk pork sausage or fresh chorizo sausage over medium heat, stirring occasionally, until no longer pink; drain, reserving drippings. Substitute drippings for part of the butter. Add cooked sausage with remaining stuffing ingredients.

WILD RICE STUFFING: Omit all ingredients. In ungreased 2-quart casserole, mix 3 cups cooked wild rice, ¼ cup melted butter, 1 cup orange juice, 1 medium apple, peeled and cut into chunks, 1 cup dry bread crumbs and ½ cup each raisins and walnuts. Cover; bake at 325°F 55 to 60 minutes or until apple is tender.

Loved by our fans with good reason. Betty takes the intimidation out of gravy making with this simple recipe and clever tricks to make it turn out perfectly every time!

Foolproof Turkey Gravy

PREP TIME: 5 Minutes | START TO FINISH: 10 Minutes | *2 cups gravy (16 servings, 2 tablespoons each)*

Turkey drippings (fat and juices from roasted turkey)

¼ cup all-purpose flour

2 cups liquid (juices from roasted turkey, broth or water)

½ teaspoon salt, or less if using turkey drippings

½ teaspoon pepper

Additional pepper, if desired

1 SERVING Calories 40; Total Fat 3.5g (Saturated Fat 1g, Trans Fat 0g); Cholesterol 0mg; Sodium 190mg; Total Carbohydrate 2g (Dietary Fiber 0g); Protein 0g **CARBOHYDRATE CHOICES:** 0

1 Pour drippings from roasting pan into bowl, leaving brown particles in pan. Return ¼ cup drippings to roasting pan. Stir in flour. Pour remaining drippings into fat separator. Pour drippings (leaving fat in separator) into 2-cup measure. Add enough broth to equal 2 cups.

2 Cook over medium heat, stirring constantly, until mixture is smooth and bubbly. Stir in 2 cups liquid. Heat to boiling, stirring constantly. Boil and stir 1 minute. Stir in salt and pepper. Pour into gravy boat or small heatproof pitcher; sprinkle with additional pepper. Serve warm.

Betty's Kitchen Tips: If you'd like a thicker gravy, mix 1 tablespoon all-purpose flour with 2 tablespoons additional broth or water, then whisk it into the hot gravy, bring to a boil, stirring constantly, and cook 1 minute longer.

Betty's Kitchen Tips: End up with a few lumps? Pour the gravy through fine-mesh strainer to give gravy a silky smoothness.

Betty's Kitchen Tips: A flavorful broth is a traditional liquid for many gravies, but you can mix things up by using wine, milk, or half-and-half with broth. Also, taste your gravy before you serve it to make sure it is well seasoned. If it's too salty, stir in a little more water or low-sodium chicken broth.

Betty's been on the scene helping folks solve cooking problems for generations. This recipe makes the cut for the clever use of leftover turkey, sweet potatoes *and* gravy.

Turkey Leftovers Pot Pie

PREP TIME: 30 Minutes | START TO FINISH: 1 Hour 5 Minutes | *6 servings*

Two-Crust Pastry (page 243) or 1 box refrigerated pie crusts, softened as directed on box

3 cups cut-up cooked turkey

2 cups loosely packed fresh baby spinach leaves (from 6-oz bag)

1¼ cups cubed (½ inch) cooked dark-orange sweet potato (about 1 small; ½ lb sweet potato)

1 cup leftover turkey gravy or jarred turkey gravy (from 12-oz jar)

½ cup sweetened dried cranberries

1 teaspoon milk

1 Heat oven to 425°F.

2 Prepare pastry as directed in Steps 2 through 4 of Classic Apple Pie—except roll each round into 12-inch circle. Place one circle in ungreased 9- or 10-inch deep-dish pie plate or shallow 2-quart casserole dish; gently press in bottom and up side of pie plate. Do not stretch.

3 In medium bowl, mix all remaining ingredients except milk; pour mixture into pastry-lined pie plate. Top with second pastry circle; seal edge and flute. Brush top crust with milk. Cut several slits in top crust for steam to escape.

4 Bake 25 to 30 minutes or until golden brown. Cool 5 minutes before serving.

1 SERVING Calories 500; Total Fat 24g (Saturated Fat 9g, Trans Fat 0g); Cholesterol 70mg; Sodium 740mg; Total Carbohydrate 50g (Dietary Fiber 2g); Protein 23g **CARBOHYDRATE CHOICES:** 3

CHICKEN-CRANBERRY POT PIE: Prepare as directed—except substitute chicken and chicken gravy for turkey and turkey gravy. Omit cooked sweet potato. Heat 1 cup chicken broth to boiling in 3-quart saucepan. Add 1½ cups cubed (½ inch) dark-orange sweet potato. Reduce heat, cover and simmer about 6 minutes or until sweet potato is almost tender. Drain; add to filling. Pour into pastry-lined pie plate and proceed with recipe.

Betty's Kitchen Tips: Use cut-up cooked turkey instead of the chicken, and leftover sweet potatoes and gravy, for another delicious twist on the Chicken Pot Pie on page 112.

Betty Crocker has worked out all the ways to customize this crust, whether you want to make it ahead or make a thin or thick crust. Top it with our delicious topping suggestions below, or create your own.

Meat Lover's Pizza

PREP TIME: 30 Minutes | **START TO FINISH:** 50 Minutes | *1 pizza (8 slices each)*

PIZZA CRUST

- 1¼ to 1½ cups all-purpose, bread or whole wheat flour
- 1½ teaspoons sugar
- ½ teaspoon salt
- 1¼ teaspoons regular active or fast-acting dry yeast
- 1 tablespoon plus 1½ teaspoons olive or vegetable oil
- ½ cup very warm water (120°F to 130°F)

TOPPING

- 1 lb ground beef (at least 80% lean)
- 1 medium onion, chopped (1 cup)
- 1 can (8 oz) pizza sauce
- 1 cup diced or sliced pepperoni
- 2 cups pizza cheese blend (8 oz)

1 In medium bowl, mix ½ cup of the flour, the sugar, salt and yeast. Add oil and warm water. Beat with electric mixer on medium speed 3 minutes, scraping bowl frequently. Stir in enough remaining flour, ½ cup at a time, until dough is soft and leaves side of bowl. Place dough on lightly floured surface; knead 5 to 8 minutes or until dough is smooth and springy.

2 Spray large bowl with cooking spray or grease with shortening. Place dough in greased bowl; cover with plastic wrap; let rest 15 minutes.

3 Meanwhile, heat oven, shape crust and partially bake for desired crust as directed in Customizable Crusts (right). In 10-inch skillet, cook ground beef and onion, stirring occasionally, until no longer pink; drain.

4 Spread pizza sauce over partially baked crust. Top sauce with ground beef mixture, pepperoni and cheese.

5 Bake thin-crust pizza 8 to 10 minutes longer, thick-crust pizza about 20 minutes longer, or until cheese is melted. Cut into slices to serve.

1 SLICE Calories 400; Total Fat 24g (Saturated Fat 10g, Trans Fat 0.5g); Cholesterol 75mg; Sodium 750mg; Total Carbohydrate 21g (Dietary Fiber 1g); Protein 22g **CARBOHYDRATE CHOICES:** 1½

CUSTOMIZABLE CRUSTS: Thin Crust Heat oven to 425°F. Grease cookie sheet or 12-inch pizza pan with oil. Sprinkle with cornmeal. Pat dough into 12-inch round on cookie sheet using floured fingers. Partially bake 7 to 8 minutes or until crust just begins to brown. Continue as directed in Step 4. **Thick Crust** Move oven rack to lowest position. Heat oven to 375°F. Grease 8-inch square or 9-inch round cake pan with oil. Sprinkle with cornmeal. Pat dough in bottom of pan using floured fingers. Partially bake 20 to 22 minutes or until crust just begins to brown. Continue as directed in Step 4.

CHEESY VEGETABLE PIZZA: Prepare as directed— except omit beef, onion, pepperoni and pizza cheese blend. In Step 4, spread partially baked pizza crust with pizza sauce. Top sauce with ½ bell pepper, sliced, half of 8-oz package sliced mushrooms, 2 tablespoons sliced fresh basil leaves and 2 cups shredded mozzarella cheese. Bake as directed.

Continues

Meat Lover's Pizza *continued*

BARBECUE CHEESEBURGER PIZZA: Prepare as directed—except substitute 1½ cups barbecue sauce for pizza sauce. Omit pepperoni. Substitute 5 slices process American cheese, cut diagonally in half, for pizza cheese. Stir ½ cup of the barbecue sauce into cooked beef mixture in Step 4. Spread remaining barbecue sauce on partially baked crust. Top with beef mixture and pickle slices, if desired. Arrange cheese slices over toppings. Bake as directed.

Make Ahead: Prepare the dough ahead, omitting rising time in Step 2; instead, refrigerate up to 24 hours. Remove from refrigerator 1 hour before shaping crust. You can also double the dough ingredients to make two different pizzas or to make one the next day: Use 2½ to 3 cups flour, 1 tablespoon sugar, 1 teaspoon salt, 1 package (2¼ teaspoons) yeast, 3 tablespoons oil and 1 cup water.

Our original meat loaf recipe first appeared in the 1950 *Betty Crocker Picture Cookbook.* "I have relied on Betty Crocker recipes for 40 years . . . the messiest pages [of my Betty Crocker cookbook include] . . . Meat Loaf."

Meat Loaf

PREP TIME: 20 Minutes | START TO FINISH: 1 Hour 40 Minutes | *6 servings*

1½ lb ground beef (at least 80% lean)
1 cup milk
1 tablespoon Worcestershire sauce
½ teaspoon salt
½ teaspoon ground mustard
¼ teaspoon pepper

1 egg, beaten
3 slices bread, finely chopped (1½ cups lightly packed)
¼ cup chopped onion
½ cup ketchup, chili sauce or barbecue sauce

 Heat oven to 350°F.

 In large bowl, mix all ingredients except ketchup. Spread mixture in ungreased 9×5-inch loaf pan, or shape into 9×5-inch loaf in ungreased 13×9-inch pan. Spread ketchup over top. Insert ovenproof meat thermometer so tip is in center of loaf.

 Bake uncovered 1 hour to 1 hour 15 minutes or until thermometer reads at least 160°F.

 Pour off fat from meat loaf and discard. Let stand 5 minutes. Remove from pan.

1 SERVING Calories 290; Total Fat 15g (Saturated Fat 6g, Trans Fat 0.5g); Cholesterol 105mg; Sodium 570mg; Total Carbohydrate 16g (Dietary Fiber 0g); Protein 23g **CARBOHYDRATE CHOICES:** 1

RECIPE

#46

Impossibly Easy Cheeseburger Pie

PREP TIME: 15 Minutes | START TO FINISH: 40 Minutes | *6 servings*

1 lb ground beef (at least 80% lean)

1 medium onion, chopped (1 cup)

½ teaspoon salt

1 cup shredded cheddar cheese (4 oz)

1 cup milk

½ cup Original Bisquick mix

2 eggs

1 Heat oven to 400°F. Grease 9-inch glass pie plate with shortening or cooking spray.

2 In 10-inch skillet, cook beef and onion over medium heat 8 to 10 minutes, stirring occasionally, until beef is browned; drain and return to skillet. Stir in salt. Spread in pie plate. Sprinkle with cheese.

3 In small bowl, mix remaining ingredients with fork or whisk until blended. Pour batter over ingredients in pie plate.

4 Bake 23 to 25 minutes or until knife inserted in center comes out clean. Let stand 5 minutes before serving. Cut into wedges.

1 SERVING Calories 300; Total Fat 19g (Saturated Fat 9g, Trans Fat 1g); Cholesterol 130mg; Sodium 510mg; Total Carbohydrate 11g (Dietary Fiber 0g); Protein 22g **CARBOHYDRATE CHOICES:** 1

GLUTEN-FREE IMPOSSIBLY EASY CHEESEBURGER PIE: Prepare as directed—except substitute 1 cup Gluten Free Bisquick mix for Original Bisquick mix and increase eggs to 3. Increase bake time to 25 to 30 minutes.

Cooking Gluten Free? Always read labels to make sure *each* recipe ingredient is gluten free. Products and ingredient sources can change.

Betty's Kitchen Tips: Top off this delicious pie just like you would a cheeseburger. Serve with barbecue sauce, bacon, sliced pickles or sliced tomato. Or go wild with pineapple slices or avocado!

Make Ahead: Cover and refrigerate the unbaked pie up to 24 hours before baking. You may need to bake a bit longer than the recipe directs since you'll be starting with a cold pie. Watch carefully for doneness.

When you crave a good old-fashioned pot roast, this is where to turn. "This is the first thing I made for my husband when we were dating in 1979, and it's still his favorite version of pot roast. Thanks, Betty Crocker."

New England Pot Roast

PREP TIME: 30 Minutes | START TO FINISH: 4 Hours | *8 servings*

- 1 boneless beef chuck arm, shoulder or blade pot roast (4 lb)
- 1 to 2 teaspoons salt
- 1 teaspoon pepper
- 1 jar (8 oz) white prepared horseradish
- 1 cup water
- 8 small potatoes, cut in half
- 8 medium carrots, cut into quarters
- 8 small onions, peeled
- ½ cup cold water
- ¼ cup all-purpose flour
- Fresh parsley, if desired

1 In 4-quart Dutch oven, cook roast over medium heat until brown on all sides. Reduce heat to low.

2 Sprinkle roast with salt and pepper. Spread horseradish over all sides of roast. Add 1 cup water to Dutch oven. Heat to boiling; reduce heat. Cover; simmer 2 hours 30 minutes.

3 Add potatoes, carrots and onions to Dutch oven. Cover; simmer about 1 hour or until roast and vegetables are tender.

4 Remove roast and vegetables to warm platter; keep warm. Skim excess fat from liquid in Dutch oven. Add enough water to liquid to measure 2 cups. In tightly covered container, shake ½ cup cold water and the flour; gradually stir into liquid. Heat to boiling, stirring constantly. Boil and stir 1 minute. Serve gravy with roast and vegetables. Garnish with parsley.

1 SERVING Calories 600; Total Fat 24g (Saturated Fat 9g, Trans Fat 1g); Cholesterol 125mg; Sodium 560mg; Total Carbohydrate 48g (Dietary Fiber 7g); Protein 47g **CARBOHYDRATE CHOICES:** 3

SLOW-COOKER POT ROAST: In 12-inch skillet, cook roast over medium heat until brown on all sides. In 4- to 6-quart slow-cooker insert, place potatoes, carrots and onions. Place roast on vegetables. In small bowl, mix horseradish, salt and pepper; spread evenly over roast. Add 1 cup water. Cover; cook on Low heat setting 8 to 10 hours or until roast and vegetables are tender. Continue as directed in Step 4—except change heat to High heat setting. Stir flour mixture into pot roast liquid in slow cooker. Cover and cook 10 to 15 minutes or until thickened.

CREAM GRAVY POT ROAST: Prepare as directed—except substitute 1 can (10.5 oz) condensed beef broth for 1 cup water. For gravy in Step 4, instead of water, add enough half-and-half or milk to cooking liquid to measure 2 cups. Substitute ½ cup half-and-half or milk for ½ cup cold water.

Betty's Kitchen Tips: You'll find prepared horseradish in glass jars in the condiment section of your supermarket.

Betty's Kitchen Tips: To carve the roast, place on carving board or serving platter so meat grain runs parallel to carving board. Holding meat in place with meat fork, cut meat across grain into ¼-inch-thick slices.

Originally in the first "Big Red," Swedish meatballs are a timeless recipe that our fans still love today. Follow our variation starting with frozen meatballs to get dinner on the table in no time.

Swedish Meatballs

PREP TIME: 1 Hour 10 Minutes | **START TO FINISH:** 1 Hour 10 Minutes | *6 servings (about 4 meatballs and ⅓ cup sauce)*

MEATBALLS

- 1 lb ground beef (at least 80% lean)
- ½ lb ground pork
- ¾ cup plain panko crispy bread crumbs
- ½ cup milk
- 2 tablespoons finely chopped fresh parsley
- 1 teaspoon Worcestershire sauce
- ½ teaspoon salt
- ⅛ teaspoon pepper
- 1 small onion, finely chopped (½ cup)
- 1 egg

GRAVY

- ¼ cup butter
- ¼ cup all-purpose flour
- 1 teaspoon paprika
- ¼ teaspoon salt
- ⅛ teaspoon pepper
- 2 cups water
- ¾ cup sour cream

1 SERVING Calories 430; Total Fat 29g (Saturated Fat 14g, Trans Fat 1g); Cholesterol 140mg; Sodium 490mg; Total Carbohydrate 17g (Dietary Fiber 0g); Protein 25g **CARBOHYDRATE CHOICES:** 1

EASY SWEDISH MEATBALLS: Prepare as directed—except substitute 1 package (24 oz) frozen meatballs or turkey meatballs for the meatballs. Heat as directed on package. Continue as directed in Step 2.

1 In large bowl, mix meatball ingredients until well blended. Shape into 1½-inch meatballs. In 12-inch skillet, cook meatballs over medium heat 8 to 10 minutes or until browned. Remove meatballs from skillet to heatproof plate; cover to keep warm. Drain fat from skillet, leaving browned bits in pan.

2 In same skillet, melt butter over medium heat. With wire whisk, stir in flour, paprika, salt and pepper until bubbly. Slowly add water, stirring constantly over medium heat until mixture boils and thickens. Add meatballs to gravy. Cook over medium-low heat 8 to 10 minutes or until meatballs are thoroughly cooked. Stir in sour cream until blended and hot.

Betty Crocker's Cooking School of the Air

In one of the longest-running network radio shows of any kind in the United States, Betty Crocker took to the airwaves across the country with a cooking program that lasted nearly 30 years. Every week, Betty Crocker would broadcast recipes, baking hints and household tips. Listeners were "enrolled" by requesting the recipes. Homework was preparing the recipes and writing a report. Those who completed all recipes and lessons "graduated" during a broadcast ceremony and received a certificate. The program was a huge hit, with more than 200 graduates in the first class. In addition to the homemakers who tuned into the program, there was a surprising additional audience—men! Many men who came home from war tuned in for the warm, friendly sounding voice . . . and Betty received four or five marriage proposals a week!

This is to certify that
Mrs. Leon Pike
has completed a course in Cooking in the
Gold Medal Flour Radio Cooking School
Signed this 2nd day of Dec. 1932
Betty Crocker
Gold Medal Flour Home Service Department
WASHBURN CROSBY COMPANY

GOOD FOOD
BROADCAST BY BETTY CROCKER FROM WCCO – OCTOBER 2, 1924

Good morning. This is a very happy morning for me because at last I have an opportunity to really talk to you. To those of you who are my friends through correspondence I wish to extend most cordial greetings and good wishes, and to those of you who are making the acquaintance of Betty Crocker for the first time - I bid you welcome to our circle.

This hour - 10:45 every morning - is yours and I am here to be of service to you. I want to tell you some of the good things I am planning for you.

First of all - cooking lessons with recipes, menus, directions for preparing the different dishes and the reasons for the methods used. It is so much easier to do a thing if we understand the reason or principle back of it.

Perhaps you are one of the fortunate few who can be rightly called "born cooks". If so I should never presume to give you instructions but it may be that you are in need of new ideas and from my contact with women all over the country I may be able to give you new suggestions that will add zest to your work.

Or it may be that you are a young housekeeper eager to learn the hows and whys and wherefores of this big job of cooking for your husband. There are many ways in which I can be of service to you, not only through cooking lessons but with suggestions for serving, for planning your housework, for marketing so that you can get the most for your money. Perhaps I can even help you with your weekly washing or tell you how to remove stains from your best tablecloth, or give you some good suggestions for housecleaning.

From time to time we shall take up a series of talks on such subjects as canning and preserving, baking, party plans and meals for special occasions.

In making my plan for you I discovered that most of the holidays this fall come on Thursday so I have chosen Thursday for party day. Every Thursday

RECIPE
#49

Slow-Cooker Pulled Pork Barbecue Sandwiches

PREP TIME: 20 Minutes | **START TO FINISH:** 10 Hours 20 Minutes | *12 sandwiches*

- 1 large onion, sliced
- 4 cloves garlic, thinly sliced
- 2 tablespoons packed brown sugar
- 1 tablespoon paprika
- 1½ teaspoons salt
- 1½ teaspoons ground mustard
- 1 teaspoon finely crushed dried chipotle chile
- 1 boneless pork shoulder (4 to 5 lb), trimmed of fat
- 1½ to 2 cups barbecue sauce
- 12 kaiser rolls or hamburger buns, split

1 SANDWICH Calories 500; Total Fat 20g (Saturated Fat 6g, Trans Fat 0.5g); Cholesterol 95mg; Sodium 960mg; Total Carbohydrate 43g (Dietary Fiber 2g); Protein 36g **CARBOHYDRATE CHOICES:** 3

1 Spray 4- to 6-quart slow-cooker insert with cooking spray. Place onion and garlic in slow cooker.

2 In small bowl, mix together brown sugar, paprika, salt, mustard and crushed chile. Rub mixture evenly over pork. Place pork in slow cooker.

3 Cover; cook on Low heat setting 8 to 10 hours until pork is very tender and shreds easily. With slotted spoon or tongs, carefully remove pork to cutting board (discard juices and vegetables in cooker); cool slightly. Using two forks, shred pork, removing and discarding excess fat. Return meat to slow cooker. Stir in enough barbecue sauce to make pork saucy. Cover; cook on High heat setting 45 minutes or until hot.

4 Spoon pork into rolls. Serve with additional barbecue sauce, if desired.

MEXICAN GARLIC-LIME SHREDDED PORK: Prepare as directed—except omit rub ingredients in Step 2 and instead rub pork with mixture of 1 tablespoon chili powder, 2 teaspoons ground cumin, 2 teaspoons dried oregano leaves, 1½ teaspoons salt and 1½ teaspoons finely crushed dried chipotle chile. Skim off fat from juices in slow cooker. Strain cooking liquid; reserve ½ cup cooking liquid and discard onions and garlic. After shredding and returning pork to slow cooker, substitute 1 cup orange juice and ¼ cup lime juice for barbecue sauce. Stir in reserved cooking liquid.

ORANGE-THYME PULLED PORK: Prepare as directed—except omit brown sugar, paprika, ground mustard and finely crushed chipotle chile. Mix in 1 teaspoon each grated orange peel and dried thyme leaves and 2 chopped green onions with the salt and pepper. Brush pork with 1 to 2 tablespoons balsamic vinegar before rubbing with orange mixture.

MAPLE-BOURBON BBQ PULLED PORK: Prepare as directed—except stir 2 tablespoons each real maple syrup and bourbon into barbecue sauce before stirring into pork.

Continues

Slow-Cooker Pulled Pork Barbecue Sandwiches *continued*

PULLED PORK AND SLAW SANDWICHES:
Top pork on buns with your favorite coleslaw before placing bun tops on sandwiches.

Betty's Kitchen Tips: Always keep your slow cooker covered for the time stated in the recipe. Each time you remove the cover, you allow heat to escape, adding 15 to 20 minutes to the cook time.

Betty's Kitchen Tips: The onion slices are used in this recipe to lift the meat away from the bottom of the slow cooker so that the fat can melt into them during cooking. For the best pork flavor and texture, we recommend discarding the cooked onions as they can add greasiness to the shredded pork, as well as dilute the flavor.

Pulled Pork and Slaw
Sandwiches

RECIPE

#50

Slow-Cooker Barbecue Beef Short Ribs

PREP TIME: 20 Minutes | START TO FINISH: 8 Hours 20 Minutes | *6 servings*

- 4 to 4½ lb bone-in beef short ribs, cut into individual ribs
- ½ teaspoon salt
- ½ teaspoon pepper
- ½ cup beef-flavored broth (from 32-oz carton)
- ¾ cup barbecue sauce
- 2 tablespoons whole grain mustard
- Sliced green onions, if desired
- Mashed potatoes, if desired

1 SERVING Calories 270; Total Fat 16g (Saturated Fat 6g, Trans Fat 0.5g); Cholesterol 80mg; Sodium 730mg; Total Carbohydrate 11g (Dietary Fiber 1g); Protein 21g **CARBOHYDRATE CHOICES:** 1

Betty's Kitchen Tips: For this recipe, ask your butcher for traditional English-style short ribs instead of the thinner Korean-style short ribs.

Betty's Kitchen Tips: To cut into individual ribs, cut between the sections, so each rib has one bone in it.

1 Spray 5- to 6-quart slow-cooker insert with cooking spray. Heat 12-inch nonstick skillet over medium-high heat. Season short ribs with salt and pepper. Cook short ribs in two batches, 2 to 3 minutes per side, until browned on all sides. Transfer short ribs to slow cooker; discard fat and drippings.

2 In small bowl, mix broth, ½ cup of the barbecue sauce and the mustard. Pour over short ribs in slow cooker. Cover; cook on Low heat setting 8 to 9 hours or until tender.

3 With slotted spoon or tongs, carefully remove short ribs to serving platter (discard juices and fat in cooker). In small microwavable bowl, heat remaining ¼ cup barbecue sauce, covered, on High 30 to 60 seconds or until heated through. Brush short ribs with remaining ¼ cup barbecue sauce; garnish with onions. Serve with mashed potatoes.

A well-seasoned pork chop that is also tender to eat might be daunting to some, but we've figured out how to achieve both in the Betty Crocker Kitchens with this recipe. It's a good one for the meal rotation!

Panfried Pork Chops with Cider Sauce

PREP TIME: 25 Minutes | START TO FINISH: 25 Minutes | *4 servings*

4 boneless pork loin chops, ½- to ¾-inch-thick, trimmed of fat

¼ teaspoon seasoned salt

¼ teaspoon dried thyme leaves

⅛ teaspoon garlic powder

⅛ teaspoon pepper

1 tablespoon vegetable oil

½ cup apple cider

¼ cup brandy or additional apple cider

1 tablespoon butter

Additional fresh thyme, if desired

1 Sprinkle both sides of pork chops with seasoned salt, thyme, garlic powder and pepper. In 12-inch skillet, heat oil over medium-high heat. Add pork; cook about 5 minutes or until bottoms are browned.

2 Turn pork chops; reduce heat to medium-low. Cook uncovered 5 to 10 minutes longer or until instant-read meat thermometer inserted in center reads 145°F for medium-rare. Remove from skillet to plate; cover with foil to keep warm.

3 Add cider and brandy to skillet. Heat to boiling, stirring to loosen browned bits from bottom of skillet; reduce heat to low. Add butter; simmer 1 to 3 minutes, stirring frequently, until sauce is slightly thickened. Serve sauce over pork. Garnish with additional thyme.

1 SERVING Calories 250; Total Fat 15g (Saturated Fat 5g, Trans Fat 0g); Cholesterol 75mg; Sodium 150mg; Total Carbohydrate 4g (Dietary Fiber 0g); Protein 24g **CARBOHYDRATE CHOICES:** 0

PORK CHOPS WITH MUSTARD-CHIVE CREAM SAUCE: Omit cider, brandy and butter. Prepare as directed through Step 2. Add ¼ cup dry sherry to skillet. Heat to boiling, stirring to loosen browned bits from bottom of skillet. Stir in ½ cup whipping cream, 1 tablespoon country-style Dijon mustard, 2 teaspoons chopped fresh chives, ⅛ teaspoon salt and ⅛ teaspoon pepper. Simmer 3 minutes, stirring frequently, until slightly thickened. Serve sauce over chops. Sprinkle with additional thyme.

SPICY SOUTHWESTERN PORK CHOPS: Omit all ingredients except pork chops. In small bowl, mix 1 teaspoon chili powder, 1 teaspoon finely crushed chipotle chile, ½ teaspoon ground cumin, ¼ teaspoon salt, ¼ teaspoon ground red pepper (cayenne), ¼ teaspoon garlic powder and ⅛ teaspoon black pepper. Rub on both sides of pork. Cook as directed in Step 2. (Pork will get very dark from spice coating.)

Betty's Kitchen Tips: Bone-in pork loin chops, ½-inch thick, can be substituted for boneless chops. Cook about 5 minutes on each side or until browned. Reduce heat to low. Cover; cook about 10 minutes longer or until pork is no longer pink in center.

RECIPE

#52

Slow-Cooker Lasagna

PREP TIME: 35 Minutes | START TO FINISH: 8 Hours 35 Minutes | *8 servings*

- ¾ lb bulk Italian sausage
- 1 small onion, chopped (½ cup)
- 2 cans (15 oz each) Italian-style tomato sauce
- 2 teaspoons dried basil leaves
- ½ teaspoon salt
- 3 cups shredded mozzarella cheese (12 oz)
- 1 container (15 oz) part-skim ricotta cheese
- 1 cup grated Parmesan cheese
- 12 uncooked lasagna noodles (12 oz)

1 SERVING Calories 570; Total Fat 26g (Saturated Fat 13g, Trans Fat 0.5g); Cholesterol 80mg; Sodium 1400mg; Total Carbohydrate 49g (Dietary Fiber 4g); Protein 35g **CARBOHYDRATE CHOICES:** 3

Betty's Kitchen Tips: For the prettiest presentation, use a 3½-quart slow cooker. You'll have thicker lasagna pieces.

Betty's Kitchen Tips: Dress up servings of this family favorite with more grated Parmesan and fresh thyme or basil leaves.

1 In 10-inch skillet, cook sausage and onion over medium heat 6 to 8 minutes, stirring occasionally, until sausage is no longer pink. Drain; return to skillet. Stir in tomato sauce, basil and salt.

2 In medium bowl, mix 2 cups of the mozzarella cheese, the ricotta cheese and Parmesan cheese.

3 Spray 3½- to 5-quart slow-cooker insert with cooking spray. Spoon one-fourth of the sausage mixture into slow cooker; top with 4 noodles, broken into pieces to fit. Top with half of the cheese mixture and another one-fourth of the sausage mixture. Top with 4 noodles, remaining cheese mixture and another one-fourth of the sausage mixture. Top with remaining 4 noodles and remaining sausage mixture.

4 Cover; cook on Low heat setting 6 to 8 hours or until noodles are tender.

5 Sprinkle top of lasagna with remaining 1 cup mozzarella cheese. Cover; let stand about 10 minutes or until cheese is melted. Cut into pieces.

RECIPE

#53

Bacon-Wrapped Barbecue Pork Tenderloin

PREP TIME: 20 Minutes | **START TO FINISH:** 1 Hour 5 Minutes | *8 servings*

8 slices bacon
2 pork tenderloins (about 1 lb each)
½ teaspoon salt
¼ teaspoon pepper

⅓ cup barbecue sauce
1 tablespoon finely chopped chipotle chile in adobo sauce
¼ teaspoon ground cumin

1 SERVING Calories 200; Total Fat 8g (Saturated Fat 2.5g, Trans Fat 0g); Cholesterol 75mg; Sodium 460mg; Total Carbohydrate 4g (Dietary Fiber 0g); Protein 28g **CARBOHYDRATE CHOICES:** 0

Betty's Kitchen Tips: Partially precooking bacon in the microwave ensures the bacon will get nice and crispy in the time it takes for tenderloin to cook.

1 Heat oven to 425°F. Line 15×10×1-inch pan with heavy-duty foil; spray foil with cooking spray.

2 Microwave bacon between layers of microwavable paper towels on microwavable plate 3 to 4 minutes or just until edges begin to brown but bacon is still soft and pliable. Cut each piece in half crosswise.

3 Season tenderloins with salt and pepper; place in pan. Arrange bacon pieces diagonally over top of pork, pressing bacon over sides. In small bowl, mix barbecue sauce, chipotle chile and cumin. Brush tops of each tenderloin with glaze.

4 Bake tenderloins 30 to 35 minutes or until instant-read meat thermometer inserted in center of pork reads 145°F. Let stand 10 minutes before slicing.

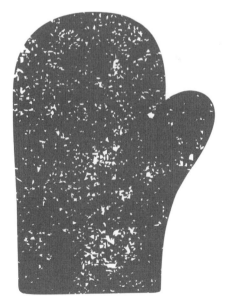

Whether because it's "penny wise," it uses ingredients you have on hand, or you're looking for something hot and hearty, this recipe takes the prize *and* honorable mention for being gluten free. To make the original (not gluten-free) recipe, simply substitute rotini for the brown rice spirals.

Gluten-Free Cheesy Tuna-Noodle Casserole

PREP TIME: 20 Minutes | START TO FINISH: 45 Minutes | *4 servings*

3 cups uncooked gluten-free brown rice pasta spirals

6 medium green onions, thinly sliced

1 small onion, finely chopped (½ cup)

½ cup frozen (thawed) sweet peas

½ teaspoon salt

¼ teaspoon pepper

1 can (18 oz) ready-to-serve creamy mushroom soup

1 can (12 oz) tuna in water, drained

1½ cups shredded sharp or regular cheddar cheese (6 oz)

1 cup coarsely crushed gluten-free potato chips

Additional sliced green onions, if desired

1 Heat oven to 400°F. Cook and drain pasta as directed on package.

2 Reserve 2 tablespoons of the green onions. In ungreased 2-quart casserole, stir together all ingredients except pasta, potato chips and reserved green onions. Gently stir in pasta.

3 Bake uncovered 25 to 30 minutes or until hot and bubbly. Sprinkle with potato chips and reserved green onions during last 5 minutes of baking. Sprinkle with additional green onions.

1 SERVING Calories 560; Total Fat 26g (Saturated Fat 12g, Trans Fat 0g); Cholesterol 65mg; Sodium 1420mg; Total Carbohydrate 50g (Dietary Fiber 3g); Protein 32g **CARBOHYDRATE CHOICES:** 3

Cooking Gluten Free? Always read labels to make sure *each* recipe ingredient is gluten free. Products and ingredient sources can change.

This staple has appeared in some fashion in most, if not all, "Big Red" cookbooks. While we've found a few ingredients to enhance the cheesiness (dry mustard and Worcestershire), it has been around since first appearing in the Supper Dish chapter in the 1950 edition.

Macaroni and Cheese

PREP TIME: 25 Minutes | START TO FINISH: 50 Minutes | *4 servings (1 cup each)*

- 1 package (7 oz) elbow macaroni (1¾ cups)
- ¼ cup butter
- ¼ cup all-purpose flour
- ½ teaspoon salt
- ¼ teaspoon pepper
- ¼ teaspoon ground mustard
- ¼ teaspoon Worcestershire sauce
- 2 cups milk or half-and-half
- 2 cups shredded sharp cheddar cheese (8 oz)

1 SERVING Calories 630; Total Fat 34g (Saturated Fat 20g, Trans Fat 1g); Cholesterol 95mg; Sodium 820mg; Total Carbohydrate 56g (Dietary Fiber 2g); Protein 25g **CARBOHYDRATE CHOICES:** 4

1 Heat oven to 350°F. Cook and drain macaroni as directed on package, using minimum cook time.

2 Meanwhile, in 3-quart saucepan, melt butter over low heat. Stir in flour, salt, pepper, mustard and Worcestershire sauce. Cook over low heat, stirring constantly, until mixture is smooth and bubbly; remove from heat.

3 Stir in milk. Heat to boiling, stirring constantly. Boil and stir 1 minute; remove from heat. Stir in cheese until melted. Gently stir macaroni into cheese sauce. Pour into ungreased 2-quart casserole.

4 Bake uncovered 20 to 25 minutes or until bubbly.

BARBECUE PULLED PORK MAC AND CHEESE: Prepare as directed—except heat oven to 375°F. Spray 3-quart glass baking dish with cooking spray. Add ½ teaspoon garlic powder with the pepper. In Step 3, before pouring macaroni and cheese into baking dish, spoon 4 cups cold Slow-Cooker Pulled Pork (page 137) into baking dish. Top macaroni with 1 cup shredded cheddar cheese and 1½ cups plain panko crispy bread crumbs mixed with ¼ cup melted butter. Bake 36 to 38 minutes or until mixture is bubbly (instant-read meat thermometer inserted in center reads at least 165°F) and bread crumbs are golden brown.

PULLED PORK MAC AND CHEESE SANDWICHES: Serve Barbecue Pulled Pork Mac and Cheese in potato buns.

Barbecue Pulled Pork Mac
and Cheese Sandwiches

This recipe doesn't have the years of history that many in this book do, but that's the point. It's a recent recipe developed for the way we are eating today, with less meat and more veggies. Betty Crocker is still creating recipes for the times!

Greek-Style Meatless Dinner

PREP TIME: 25 Minutes | START TO FINISH: 25 Minutes | *4 servings*

1   tablespoon olive oil
1   clove garlic, finely chopped
2   cups frozen veggie crumbles (from a 12-oz bag)
1   cup water
2   teaspoons Greek seasoning
1   can (14.5 oz) diced tomatoes, undrained
½   cup uncooked orzo or rosamarina pasta

1   can (15.5 oz) chick peas (garbanzo beans), drained, rinsed
2   cups packed fresh baby spinach leaves (from 6-oz bag)
½   cup crumbled feta cheese (2 oz)
2   tablespoons chopped red onion
2   tablespoons chopped fresh Italian (flat-leaf) parsley

1 SERVING Calories 360; Total Fat 10g (Saturated Fat 3.5g, Trans Fat 0g); Cholesterol 15mg; Sodium 1240mg; Total Carbohydrate 42g (Dietary Fiber 9g); Protein 24g **CARBOHYDRATE CHOICES:** 3

Betty's Kitchen Tips: If you can't find Greek seasoning or want to make your own, just use ½ teaspoon dried oregano leaves, ½ teaspoon dried thyme leaves, ½ teaspoon dried basil leaves and ½ teaspoon salt.

Betty's Kitchen Tips: Try using baby kale in place of the spinach. Baby kale is more delicate than mature kale and will add a slight peppery flavor to the dish.

Betty's Kitchen Tips: Top each serving with a dollop of tzatziki cucumber sauce (usually found near the refrigerated deli items at your supermarket). You can also serve this with pita bread, cut into wedges.

1 In 12-inch nonstick skillet, heat oil over medium heat. Add garlic; cook 1 minute, stirring constantly.

2 Add veggie crumbles, water, Greek seasoning and tomatoes; heat to boiling. Stir in orzo and chick peas. Heat to boiling; reduce heat to low. Cover; simmer 14 to 17 minutes, stirring once, until orzo is tender.

3 Add spinach; cook 2 to 3 minutes, stirring occasionally, until spinach is wilted. Remove from heat. Top with cheese, onion and parsley.

Irresistible Cookies, Bars and Candies

RECIPE #57

THE top-ranked recipe on bettycrocker.com! It's got the perfect ratio of ingredients, producing cookies that are a little thicker and chewier to sink your teeth into and with richer flavor than other chocolate chip cookie recipes.

Ultimate Chocolate Chip Cookies

PREP TIME: 15 Minutes | START TO FINISH: 1 Hour 30 Minutes | *4 dozen cookies*

2¼ cups all-purpose flour
1 teaspoon baking soda
½ teaspoon salt
1 cup butter, softened
¾ cup granulated sugar
¾ cup packed brown sugar

1 egg
1 teaspoon vanilla
1 bag (12 oz) semisweet chocolate chips
1 cup coarsely chopped nuts, if desired

1 COOKIE Calories 120; Total Fat 6g (Saturated Fat 3.5g, Trans Fat 0g); Cholesterol 15mg; Sodium 85mg; Total Carbohydrate 16g (Dietary Fiber 0g); Protein 1g **CARBOHYDRATE CHOICES:** 1

1 Heat oven to 375°F.

2 In small bowl, mix flour, baking soda and salt; set aside. In large bowl, beat butter, granulated sugar and brown sugar with electric mixer on medium speed, or mix with spoon about 1 minute or until fluffy, scraping bowl occasionally.

3 Beat in egg and vanilla until smooth. Stir in flour mixture just until blended (dough will be stiff). Stir in chocolate chips and nuts.

4 On ungreased cookie sheet, drop dough by rounded tablespoonfuls 2 inches apart.

5 Bake 8 to 10 minutes or until light brown (centers will be soft). Cool on cookie sheet 2 minutes; remove from cookie sheet to cooling rack. Cool cookie sheet before repeating Steps 4 and 5 for subsequent batches of cookies. Cool cookies completely, about 30 minutes.

Betty's Kitchen Tips: The best way to measure flour is to first stir the flour a bit before spooning into the measuring cup. Fill until heaping, and then sweep the excess off the top with the flat edge of a butter knife.

Betty's Kitchen Tips: Use an ice cream scoop to make consistently even-shaped cookies.

Betty's Kitchen Tips: The best cookie sheets are shiny aluminum with a smooth surface and no sides. They reflect heat, letting cookies bake evenly and brown properly. Bake one pan of cookies at a time, in the middle of the oven, for bakery-worthy results.

Betty's Kitchen Tips: Change up the nuts and chips in this recipe, and you've got yourself a brand-new cookie! Macadamia nuts and white vanilla baking chips, chopped peanuts and peanut butter chips or chopped pecans and butterscotch chips (sprinkle lightly with coarse salt before baking). Whatever you decide, just replace the chocolate chips and nuts with the same amount of new ingredients.

How to Store: Store these most-requested cookies covered in airtight container.

Choco-holics have met their match. If you take everything you love about brownies and turn it into a cookie, pure heaven is what you get! We minimize the time needed to prepare this recipe by having you toast the pecans first so they can cool while preparing the dough.

Brownie Cookies

PREP TIME: 30 Minutes | START TO FINISH: 1 Hour | *About 2½ dozen cookies*

2	cups chopped pecans, toasted, if desired
3	cups semisweet chocolate chips (18 oz)
½	cup butter, cut into pieces
4	oz unsweetened baking chocolate, chopped

1½	cups all-purpose flour
½	teaspoon baking powder
½	teaspoon salt
1½	cups sugar
2	teaspoons vanilla
4	eggs

1 COOKIE Calories 280; Total Fat 8g (Saturated Fat 4.5g, Trans Fat 0g); Cholesterol 0mg; Sodium 85mg; Total Carbohydrate 31g (Dietary Fiber 3g); Protein 4g **CARBOHYDRATE CHOICES:** 2

Betty's Kitchen Tips: To toast pecans, spread in ungreased shallow pan. Bake uncovered 6 to 10 minutes, stirring occasionally until light brown. Remove from pan to heatproof plate and set aside.

How to Store: Store these double chocolate cookies in covered container.

1 Heat oven to 350°F.

2 In 3-quart heavy saucepan, heat 1½ cups of the chocolate chips, the butter and baking chocolate over low heat, stirring constantly, until butter and chocolates are melted. Remove from heat; cool.

3 In medium bowl, mix flour, baking powder and salt; set aside. In large bowl, beat sugar, vanilla and eggs with electric mixer on medium speed until well blended. On low speed, gradually beat in flour mixture. Add chocolate mixture; beat well. Stir in pecans and remaining 1½ cups chocolate chips.

4 Line cookie sheet with cooking parchment paper. On cookie sheet, drop dough by 2 tablespoonfuls about 1 inch apart.

5 Bake 10 minutes. Cool on cookie sheet 2 minutes; remove from cookie sheet to cooling rack. Cool cookie sheet before repeating Steps 4 and 5 for subsequent batches of cookies.

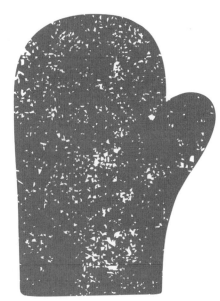

We've made our original molasses cookies chewier by changing from brown sugar to granulated, reduced the amount of shortening and took out the egg. But we didn't stop there! We also made them easier by dropping them rather than refrigerating and rolling them. And to top it off, we added a glaze for the ultimate in taste and texture!

Old-Fashioned Molasses Cookies

PREP TIME: 30 Minutes | START TO FINISH: 1 Hour 30 Minutes | *About 2 dozen cookies*

COOKIES
- 1 cup granulated sugar
- ½ cup shortening or butter, softened
- 1 cup full-flavor (dark) molasses
- ½ cup water
- 4 cups all-purpose flour
- 1½ teaspoons salt
- 1½ teaspoons ground ginger
- 1 teaspoon baking soda
- ½ teaspoon ground cloves
- ½ teaspoon ground nutmeg
- ¼ teaspoon ground allspice
- Additional granulated or sparkling sugar

ICING
- 1½ cups powdered sugar
- 1 tablespoon plus 1½ teaspoons milk
- ¼ teaspoon vanilla

1 Heat oven to 375°F. Grease cookie sheet with shortening or spray with cooking spray.

2 In large bowl, beat 1 cup granulated sugar and the shortening with electric mixer on medium speed, or mix with spoon, until well blended. Stir in remaining cookie ingredients except additional sugar until blended.

3 Shape dough by 2 tablespoonfuls into balls. Roll balls in additional granulated sugar. On cookie sheets, place balls about 1 inch apart.

4 Bake 12 to 14 minutes or until set. Cool on cookie sheet 2 minutes; remove from cookie sheets to cooling rack. Cool cookie sheet before repeating Steps 3 and 4 for subsequent batches of cookies. Cool completely.

5 Mix powdered sugar, 1 tablespoon of the milk and the vanilla until smooth. Stir in additional milk, ½ teaspoon at a time, until desired spreading consistency. Spread on cookies.

1 COOKIE Calories 220; Total Fat 4.5g (Saturated Fat 1g, Trans Fat 0g); Cholesterol 0mg; Sodium 210mg; Total Carbohydrate 42g (Dietary Fiber 0g); Protein 2g **CARBOHYDRATE CHOICES:** 3

How to Store: Let cookie icing dry to the touch before stacking cookies. Store cookies in tightly covered container.

RECIPE

#60

Snickerdoodles

PREP TIME: 40 Minutes | START TO FINISH: 50 Minutes | *About 4 dozen cookies*

1¾ cups sugar
½ cup butter, softened
½ cup shortening
2 eggs
2¾ cups all-purpose flour

2 teaspoons cream of tartar
1 teaspoon baking soda
¼ teaspoon salt
2 teaspoons ground cinnamon

1 Heat oven to 400°F.

2 In large bowl, mix 1½ cups of the sugar, the butter, shortening and eggs. Stir in flour, cream of tartar, baking soda and salt.

3 Shape dough into 1¼-inch balls. In small bowl, mix the remaining ¼ cup sugar and the cinnamon. Roll balls in cinnamon-sugar mixture. On ungreased cookie sheet, place balls 2 inches apart.

4 Bake 8 to 10 minutes or until set. Remove from cookie sheet to cooling rack. Cool cookie sheet before repeating Steps 3 and 4 for subsequent batches of cookies.

1 COOKIE Calories 90; Total Fat 4.5g (Saturated Fat 2g, Trans Fat 0g); Cholesterol 15mg; Sodium 55mg; Total Carbohydrate 13g (Dietary Fiber 0g); Protein 1g **CARBOHYDRATE CHOICES:** 1

How to Store: Snickerdoodles are best stored in a tightly covered container.

"A full cooky jar makes a home 'homey'"—Betty Crocker, 1950. Developed for *Betty Crocker's Cookie Cookbook* (2019), this new twist on an old-fashioned favorite quickly rose to the top of our treasured recipes to fill a family cookie jar.

Butter Pecan Pudding Cookies

PREP TIME: 20 Minutes | START TO FINISH: 1 Hour 30 Minutes | *4 dozen cookies*

2½ cups all-purpose flour

1½ teaspoons baking soda

½ teaspoon salt

1 cup butter, softened

1 cup packed brown sugar

½ cup granulated sugar

1 box (4-serving size) French vanilla instant pudding and pie filling mix

2 eggs

1 teaspoon vanilla

2 cups chopped pecans, toasted

½ cup toffee bits

1 Heat oven to 350°F.

2 In medium bowl, mix flour, baking soda and salt; set aside. In large bowl, beat butter, brown sugar and granulated sugar with electric mixer on medium speed until fluffy; scrape bowl. Beat in dry pudding mix. Beat in eggs, one at a time, just until smooth. Beat in vanilla. Stir in flour mixture with spoon until well mixed (dough will be stiff). Stir in pecans and toffee bits.

3 On ungreased cookie sheet, drop dough by rounded tablespoonfuls 2 inches apart. Flatten slightly.

4 Bake 8 to 10 minutes or until edges are light golden brown. Cool on cookie sheet 1 minute; remove from cookie sheet to cooling rack. Cool cookie sheet before repeating Steps 3 and 4 for subsequent batches of cookies. Cool completely, about 30 minutes.

1 COOKIE Calories 140; Total Fat 8g (Saturated Fat 3g, Trans Fat 0g); Cholesterol 20mg; Sodium 125mg; Total Carbohydrate 16g (Dietary Fiber 0g); Protein 1g **CARBOHYDRATE CHOICES:** 1

Betty's Kitchen Tips: Toasting the pecans for the cookies adds depth and richness—don't skip this step! To toast pecans, heat the oven to 350°F. Spread nuts in an ungreased shallow pan. Bake uncovered 6 to 10 minutes, stirring occasionally, until light brown. Remove from pan to heatproof plate to cool.

Betty's Kitchen Tips: Cookies will spread too much if put on hot or warm cookie sheet, so wait until it has completely cooled before dropping the next batch.

How to Store: Store cooled cookies in tightly covered container.

A top-searched, top-rated recipe on bettycrocker.com, this is loved as both a holiday cookie tray classic and lunch box treat for its delightful chocolate–peanut butter flavor and sink-your-teeth-into texture.

Peanut Butter Blossom Cookies

PREP TIME: 1 Hour | START TO FINISH: 1 Hour | *About 3 dozen cookies*

½ cup granulated sugar
½ cup packed brown sugar
½ cup creamy peanut butter
½ cup butter, softened
1 egg
1½ cups all-purpose flour

¾ teaspoon baking soda
½ teaspoon baking powder
Additional granulated sugar
About 36 milk chocolate candy drops or pieces, unwrapped

1 COOKIE Calories 120; Total Fat 6g (Saturated Fat 3g, Trans Fat 0g); Cholesterol 15mg; Sodium 75mg; Total Carbohydrate 14g (Dietary Fiber 0g); Protein 2g **CARBOHYDRATE CHOICES:** 1

Betty's Kitchen Tips: You can use coarse sugar, colored sugar, or sparkling sugar to roll the balls in; each gives a different look.

How to Store: Once the chocolate candies have completely cooled (about 2 hours), you can stack these cookies to store in a tightly covered container. Make one layer candy side up, and the next layer candy side down, between the cookies on the first layer.

1 Heat oven to 375°F.

2 In large bowl, beat ½ cup granulated sugar, the brown sugar, peanut butter, butter and egg with electric mixer on medium speed, or mix with spoon, until well blended. Stir in flour, baking soda and baking powder until dough forms.

3 Shape dough into 1-inch balls; roll in additional granulated sugar. On ungreased cookie sheets, place balls about 2 inches apart.

4 Bake 8 to 10 minutes or until edges are light golden brown. Immediately press 1 candy into center of each cookie; remove from cookie sheet to cooling rack. Cool cookie sheet before repeating Steps 3 and 4 for subsequent batches of cookies.

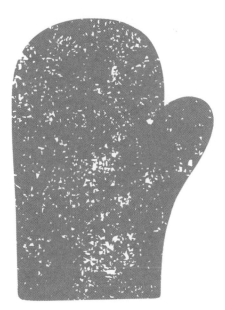

RECIPE

#63

Gluten-Free Almond Shortbread Cookies

PREP TIME: 25 Minutes | START TO FINISH: 45 Minutes | *4 dozen cookies*

- ¾ cup butter, softened
- ¼ cup granulated sugar
- 1 teaspoon almond extract
- 2 cups Betty Crocker Gluten Free all-purpose rice flour blend
- ¼ teaspoon gluten-free baking powder
- 48 almond slices (about 1 tablespoon)
- 1 tablespoon coarse sugar

1 Heat oven to 350°F.

2 In large bowl, beat butter, granulated sugar and almond extract with electric mixer on medium speed until smooth and creamy. Beat in rice flour blend and baking powder until well blended (dough will be crumbly). Shape into a ball.

3 Roll dough on lightly floured surface until ¼-inch thick. Cut with 1¾-inch round cookie cutter, rerolling if necessary. On ungreased cookie sheet, place cookies ½ inch apart. Place 1 almond slice on top of each cookie; sprinkle with coarse sugar.

4 Bake 12 to 15 minutes or until set. Cool on cookie sheet 1 minute; remove from cookie sheets to cooling rack. Cool cookie sheet before repeating Steps 3 and 4 for subsequent batches of cookies. Cool completely.

1 COOKIE Calories 50; Total Fat 3g (Saturated Fat 2g, Trans Fat 0g); Cholesterol 10mg; Sodium 50mg; Total Carbohydrate 6g (Dietary Fiber 0g); Protein 0g **CARBOHYDRATE CHOICES:** ½

VANILLA SHORTBREAD COOKIES: Prepare as directed—except substitute 1 teaspoon gluten-free vanilla for almond extract and omit sliced almonds.

Cooking Gluten Free? Always read labels to make sure *each* recipe ingredient is gluten free. Products and ingredient sources can change.

RECIPE
#64

Gluten-Free Glazed Sugar Cookies

PREP TIME: 25 Minutes | START TO FINISH: 2 Hours | *2 dozen cookies*

COOKIES

- 1 cup granulated sugar
- ½ cup shortening
- ½ cup butter, softened
- 2 teaspoons gluten-free vanilla
- 1 egg
- 2½ cups Betty Crocker Gluten Free all-purpose rice flour blend
- ½ teaspoon gluten-free baking powder
- ¼ teaspoon salt

GLAZE

- 1 cup powdered sugar
- 2 tablespoons milk

  Additional granulated sugar, if desired

1 COOKIE Calories 160; Total Fat 9g (Saturated Fat 3.5g, Trans Fat 0g); Cholesterol 20mg; Sodium 70mg; Total Carbohydrate 18g (Dietary Fiber 0g); Protein 1g **CARBOHYDRATE CHOICES:** 1

Cooking Gluten Free? Always read labels to make sure *each* recipe ingredient is gluten free. Products and ingredient sources can change.

1 In large bowl, beat sugar, shortening and butter with electric mixer on medium speed, scraping bowl often, until creamy. On low speed, beat in vanilla and egg. Stir in flour blend, baking powder and salt until well mixed. Divide dough in half; shape each half into a round. Wrap in plastic wrap; refrigerate about 1 hour or until firm.

2 Heat oven to 375°F. Roll one round of the dough on surface lightly sprinkled with flour blend until ¼-inch thick. Cut with 2½-inch cookie cutters. On ungreased cookie sheet, place cookies 1 inch apart.

3 Bake 8 to 12 minutes or until edges are lightly browned. Cool on cookie sheet 2 minutes; remove from cookie sheets to cooling rack. Repeat with other dough round. Cool completely, about 15 minutes.

4 In small bowl, stir together glaze ingredients. Drizzle glaze over cookies. Sprinkle with additional granulated sugar.

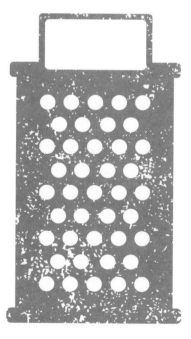

Appearing in the *Betty Crocker Cooky Cookbook* (1963) and many other cookbooks over the years, this sugar cookie recipe continues to win over taste buds with its very special homemade flavor.

Mary's Sugar Cookies

PREP TIME: 1 Hour | START TO FINISH: 4 Hours 10 Minutes | *About 5 dozen cookies*

1½ cups powdered sugar
1 cup butter, softened
1 teaspoon vanilla
½ teaspoon almond extract
1 egg
2½ cups all-purpose flour

1 teaspoon baking soda
1 teaspoon cream of tartar
Granulated or sparkling sugar, if desired

1 In large bowl, beat powdered sugar and butter with electric mixer on medium speed until well blended, or mix with spoon. Stir in vanilla, almond extract and egg. Stir in flour, baking soda and cream of tartar until well mixed. Cover; refrigerate about 2 hours or until firm.

2 Heat oven to 375°F. Roll half of dough at a time on lightly floured surface until ⅛-inch thick. Cut with 2- to 2½-inch cookie cutters into desired shapes. On ungreased cookie sheet, place cookies about 2 inches apart. Sprinkle with granulated sugar.

3 Bake 7 to 8 minutes or until light brown. Immediately remove from cookie sheets to cooling rack. Cool cookie sheet before repeating Steps 2 and 3 for subsequent batches of cookies.

1 COOKIE Calories 60; Total Fat 3g (Saturated Fat 2g, Trans Fat 0g); Cholesterol 10mg; Sodium 45mg; Total Carbohydrate 7g (Dietary Fiber 0g); Protein 0g **CARBOHYDRATE CHOICES:** ½

FRUIT-FLAVORED SUGAR COOKIES: Prepare cookies as directed—except sprinkle the cutout cookies with dry fruit-flavored gelatin instead of sugar.

Betty's Kitchen Tips: If you'd like to glaze these cookies instead of topping them with sugar, omit sprinkling sugar on cookies before baking. To glaze, make double batch (twice the amount of each ingredient called for) of Glaze (page 170). After cookies are cool, spread glaze on cookies. Sprinkle with decorator sugar or sprinkles; place dots of other colors of icing on wet glaze; drag through glaze with toothpick, or squeeze other colors of icing over wet glaze from squeeze bottle with small tip. To store, allow cookies to dry on cooling rack until no indentation remains when pressed lightly with a finger.

Make Ahead: The dough can be wrapped with plastic wrap and refrigerated up to 5 days, or place wrapped ball in resealable freezer plastic bag and freeze up to 3 months. Thaw in refrigerator and proceed with Step 2. Or freeze the baked, cooled, unglazed cookies in tightly covered container up to 12 months, or freeze glazed cookies, between layers of waxed paper, up to 3 months.

This clever recipe (with all Betty's tips and tricks) allows you to get creative any time of the year and have beautiful results. These cookies are guaranteed to wow!

Magic Window Cookies

PREP TIME: 1 Hour 55 Minutes | START TO FINISH: 3 Hours 25 Minutes | *About 6 dozen cookies*

1 cup sugar
¾ cup butter, softened
1 teaspoon vanilla
2 eggs
2½ cups all-purpose flour
1 teaspoon baking powder
¼ teaspoon salt
4 rolls (about 1 oz each) ring-shaped hard candies or about 10 other fruit-flavored hard candies, unwrapped

1 In large bowl, beat sugar, butter, vanilla and eggs with electric mixer on medium speed until well blended, or mix with spoon. Stir in flour, baking powder and salt until dough forms. Cover; refrigerate about 1 hour or until firm.

2 Heat oven to 375°F. Cover cookie sheet with cooking parchment paper or foil. Roll one-third of dough at a time on lightly floured surface until ⅛-inch thick. Cut with 3-inch cookie cutters into desired shapes. Cut desired shapes from centers of cookies. On cookie sheet, place cookies 2 inches apart.

3 Place whole or partially crushed pieces of candy in cutouts, depending on size and shape of design, mixing colors as desired. Leave pieces as large as possible because candy melts easily (do not use fine candy "dust"). Place cutouts from centers of cookies on top of candies, if desired, or bake alongside cookies.

4 Bake 7 to 9 minutes or until cookies are very light brown and candy is melted. If candy has not completely spread within cutout design, immediately spread with knife. Cool completely on cookie sheet, about 30 minutes. Gently remove from cooking parchment paper to cooling rack. Cool cookie sheet before repeating Steps 3 and 4 for subsequent batches of cookies.

1 COOKIE Calories 50; Total Fat 2g (Saturated Fat 1.5g, Trans Fat 0g); Cholesterol 10mg; Sodium 30mg; Total Carbohydrate 7g (Dietary Fiber 0g); Protein 0g **CARBOHYDRATE CHOICES:** ½

Betty's Kitchen Tips: To crush candy, place in resealable freezer plastic bag and tap lightly with rolling pin. An easy way to remove the candy "dust" is to shake candy pieces in a strainer over a bowl. Save leftover candy "dust" to sprinkle on pudding or frosted cupcakes.

A Trusted Helper *in the Kitchen*

In the early years, Betty helped homemakers stretch their wartime rations and food budgets with economical, all-family recipes. When pocketbooks were nearly empty, Betty Crocker offered hostess tips and decorating ideas for backyard bashes and birthday parties that didn't break the bank.

In recent times, Betty Crocker has offered recipes from the pantry during COVID-19 quarantining, college care package ideas, recipes for one or two, veggie-centric main dishes and gluten-free and vegan recipes. Betty shows you how to host a girls' night in and a gender reveal party, and gives you timetables for Thanksgiving Dinner. Betty Crocker products help busy families connect with delicious, homemade food.

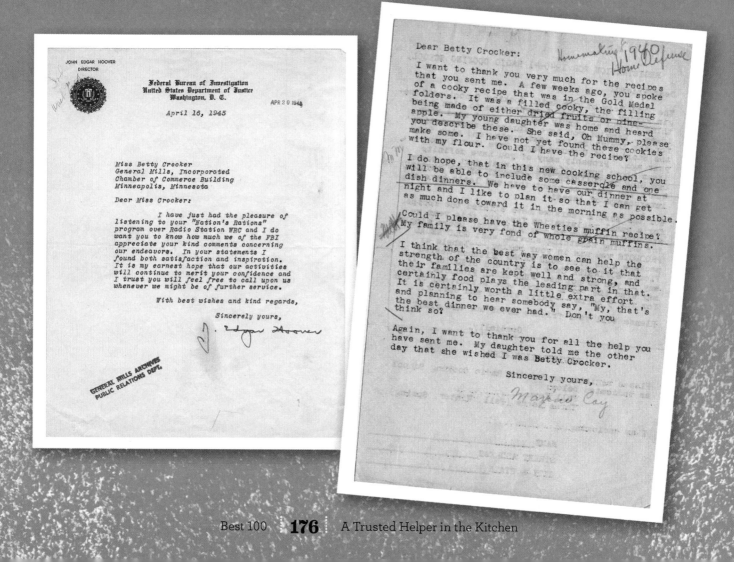

Dear Betty Crocker,

I wanted to share something positive with you all. This quarantine has been tough for everyone, especially the elderly who live in assisted living communities without much social interaction. My 92-year-old grandmother is sharp, and one of her favorite pastimes is to bake.

Each week I have been sending her groceries using various online grocery services. On a whim, I added the cinnamon streusel muffin mix to her order. She likes to bake for the other residents and staff who are working so hard during this time, and after her first time making the muffins, she called me and said that everyone was RAVING about them.

Each week, she has been politely requesting I send her more and more of the muffin mix, and she can't get enough. Lately it has not been in stock at her grocery stores, but I continue to search far and wide for them.

I just wanted to let you know how much joy you have brought to her life, and how grateful we are that she is finding new ways to occupy her time during this crazy pandemic. She is an absolute superstar, and if you saw a picture of her, you would never think she was 92. She loves to dance and sing everywhere she goes, and I can't wait to share a cinnamon streusel muffin with her when this pandemic is over!

Thank you, thank you, thank you!

Cherry Blinks is a homemade scratch version of Cherry Winks, a $5000 winner in the 1950 Pillsbury™ Bake-Off®, which used refrigerated cookie dough as the base. Betty Crocker's version uses Wheaties® and candied cherries.

Cherry Blinks

PREP TIME: 40 Minutes | START TO FINISH: 40 Minutes | *About 3 dozen cookies*

1¾ cups Wheaties cereal
½ cup sugar
⅓ cup shortening
1 tablespoon plus 1½ teaspoons milk
1 teaspoon vanilla
1 egg
1 cup all-purpose flour

½ teaspoon baking powder
¼ teaspoon baking soda
¼ teaspoon salt
½ cup raisins
½ cup chopped nuts
About 36 candied or maraschino cherries

1 Heat oven to 375°F. Crush cereal; set aside.

2 In large bowl, mix sugar, shortening, milk, vanilla and egg until well blended. Stir in flour, baking powder, baking soda and salt until dough forms. Stir in raisins and nuts.

3 Drop dough by teaspoonfuls into crushed cereal; roll gently until completely coated. On ungreased cookie sheets, place cookies about 2 inches apart. Press cherry into each cookie.

4 Bake 10 to 12 minutes or just until set. Immediately remove from cookie sheets to cooling rack. Cool cookie sheet before repeating Steps 3 and 4 for subsequent batches of cookies. Cool completely.

1 COOKIE Calories 80; Total Fat 3g (Saturated Fat 0.5g, Trans Fat 0g); Cholesterol 5mg; Sodium 45mg; Total Carbohydrate 11g (Dietary Fiber 0g); Protein 1g **CARBOHYDRATE CHOICES:** 1

Betty's Kitchen Tips: To crush cereal, place it in resealable freezer plastic bag and roll with rolling pin. Shake and flatten bag occasionally to move larger cereal pieces so cereal can be crushed evenly.

Make Ahead: Cookie dough can be covered and refrigerated up to 24 hours before baking. If it's too firm to scoop, let stand at room temperature 30 minutes.

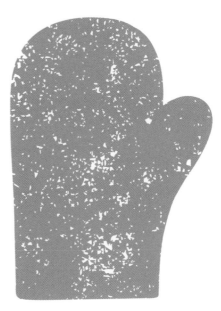

While the Girl Scouts are rumored to have created the original campfire s'mores recipe to teach cooking and campfire skills, Betty Crocker gets the credit for this clever indoor recipe, for when the weather won't permit a campfire!

Indoor S'mores

PREP TIME: 25 Minutes | START TO FINISH: 1 Hour 25 Minutes | *24 bars*

8 cups honey graham cereal squares

1 bag (10 oz) miniature marshmallows (5½ cups)

1½ cups milk chocolate chips (9 oz)

5 tablespoons butter

¼ cup sugar

1 tablespoon water

1 teaspoon vanilla

1 Grease 13×9-inch pan with butter. Place cereal in large bowl.

2 Reserve 1 cup of the marshmallows. In 3-quart saucepan, heat remaining 4½ cups marshmallows, the chocolate chips, butter, sugar and water over low heat, stirring occasionally, until completely melted. Remove from heat; stir in vanilla. Pour marshmallow mixture over cereal; stir until evenly coated. Stir in remaining 1 cup marshmallows.

3 Press firmly into pan. Cool at least 1 hour or until firm. Cut into 6 rows by 4 rows.

1 BAR Calories 180; Total Fat 6g (Saturated Fat 3.5g, Trans Fat 0g); Cholesterol 10mg; Sodium 140mg; Total Carbohydrate 31g (Dietary Fiber 1g); Protein 2g **CARBOHYDRATE CHOICES:** 2

MICROWAVE INDOOR S'MORES: Prepare as directed—except in Step 2, in large microwavable bowl, microwave remaining 4½ cups marshmallows, the chocolate chips, butter, sugar and water uncovered on High 2 minutes to 3 minutes 30 seconds, stirring after every minute, until melted and smooth when stirred. Stir in vanilla.

Betty's Kitchen Tips: If you spray your bowl with cooking spray before using it, it will be easier to mix the ingredients and you'll have less mess to clean up when you're done.

Betty's Kitchen Tips: If you prefer your marshmallows more visible in the bars, wait a minute or two after mixing the warm chocolate and marshmallow mixture into the cereal to allow it to cool slightly before you stir in the final cup of marshmallows.

How to Store: Store s'mores loosely covered at room temperature.

Brownie recipes have appeared in Betty Crocker cookbooks since the beginning. This recipe has been tweaked over the years to make it even more decadent. It still remains our favorite—you have to decide if you want to make the basic recipe or one of the irresistible variations. No matter what you choose, you and your tasters will love them!

Frosted Fudge Brownies

PREP TIME: 35 Minutes | START TO FINISH: 3 Hours 10 Minutes | *16 brownies*

BROWNIES

- ⅔ cup butter
- 5 oz unsweetened baking chocolate, chopped
- 1¾ cups granulated sugar
- 2 teaspoons vanilla
- 3 eggs
- 1 cup all-purpose flour
- ½ cup chopped walnuts, toasted if desired

FUDGE FROSTING

- 1 cup granulated sugar
- ½ cup unsweetened baking cocoa
- ½ cup milk
- ¼ cup butter, cut into pieces
- 2 tablespoons light corn syrup
- ⅛ teaspoon salt
- 1 teaspoon vanilla
- 1¼ to 1½ cups powdered sugar

1 Heat oven to 350°F. Grease bottom and sides of 9-inch square pan with shortening.

2 In 1-quart saucepan, melt butter and chocolate over low heat, stirring constantly. Cool 5 minutes.

3 In medium bowl, beat granulated sugar, vanilla and eggs with electric mixer on high speed 5 minutes, or until well blended. Beat in chocolate mixture on low speed, scraping bowl occasionally. Beat in flour just until blended, scraping bowl occasionally. Stir in walnuts. Spread in pan.

4 Bake 40 to 45 minutes or just until brownies begin to pull away from sides of pan. Cool completely in pan on cooling rack, about 2 hours.

5 Meanwhile, in 2-quart saucepan, mix all frosting ingredients except vanilla and powdered sugar. Heat to boiling, stirring frequently. Boil 3 minutes, stirring occasionally. Remove from heat; cool 45 minutes.

6 Beat in vanilla and enough powdered sugar until spreading consistency; frost brownies. Cut into 4 rows by 4 rows.

1 BROWNIE Calories 400; Total Fat 17g (Saturated Fat 10g, Trans Fat 0g); Cholesterol 65mg; Sodium 120mg; Total Carbohydrate 56g (Dietary Fiber 2g); Protein 4g **CARBOHYDRATE CHOICES:** 4

CHOCOLATE BROWNIE PIE: Prepare as directed—except grease bottom and side of 10-inch glass pie plate with shortening. Spread batter in pie plate. Bake 35 to 40 minutes or until center is set. Cool completely in pan on cooling rack. Cut into wedges. Omit frosting. Serve with ice cream and hot fudge sauce, if desired. 12 servings

CHOCOLATE–PEANUT BUTTER BROWNIES: Prepare as directed—except substitute ⅓ cup crunchy peanut butter for ⅓ cup of the butter. Omit walnuts. Before baking, arrange 16 miniature chocolate-covered peanut butter cup candies, unwrapped, on top; press into batter so tops of cups are even with top of batter.

Continues

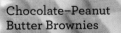
Chocolate–Peanut
Butter Brownies

Chocolate–
Peanut Butter
Brownies

Frosted Fudge Brownies continued

DOUBLE CHOCOLATE BROWNIES: Prepare as directed—except stir in ½ cup semisweet or dark chocolate chips after adding the flour in Step 3.

Betty's Kitchen Tips: To toast walnuts, heat the oven to 350°F. Spread nuts in an ungreased shallow pan. Bake uncovered 6 to 10 minutes, stirring occasionally, until light brown.

Betty's Kitchen Tips: Brownies will start to pull away from sides of pan when done.

This is one of the first recipes ever developed for our very extensive Betty Crocker Kitchens recipe database. We've made them even better with butterscotch chips inside and a fantastic butterscotch glaze that doubles the butterscotch flavor.

Double Butterscotch Brownies

PREP TIME: 15 Minutes | **START TO FINISH:** 45 Minutes | *16 brownies*

BUTTERSCOTCH BROWNIES

- ¼ cup butter
- 1 cup packed brown sugar
- 2 tablespoons milk
- 1 teaspoon vanilla
- 1 egg
- 1 cup all-purpose flour
- 1 teaspoon baking powder
- ½ teaspoon salt
- ½ cup chopped pecans
- ½ cup butterscotch chips (from 11-oz bag)

BUTTERSCOTCH GLAZE

- ¼ cup heavy whipping cream
- ⅔ cup butterscotch chips (from 11-oz bag)

Chopped pecans, if desired

1 Heat oven to 350°F. Grease bottom and sides of 8-inch square pan with shortening.

2 In 1½-quart saucepan, melt butter over low heat; remove from heat. Stir in brown sugar, milk, vanilla and egg until well mixed. Stir in flour, baking powder and salt until only small lumps remain. Stir in ½ cup pecans and ½ cup butterscotch chips. Spread in pan.

3 Bake about 25 to 30 minutes or until golden brown. Cool in pan on cooling rack 5 minutes.

4 Meanwhile, in 1-quart saucepan, heat cream over low heat just to boiling. Remove from heat; stir in ⅔ cup butterscotch chips until melted. Let stand about 15 minutes or until mixture is desired drizzling consistency.

5 Drizzle over brownies; sprinkle with chopped pecans. Cut into 4 rows by 4 rows.

1 BROWNIE Calories 220; Total Fat 11g (Saturated Fat 6g, Trans Fat 0g); Cholesterol 25mg; Sodium 150mg; Total Carbohydrate 29g (Dietary Fiber 0g); Protein 2g **CARBOHYDRATE CHOICES:** 2

Our fans love our recipes that combine chocolate with salted caramel or salty pretzels. This recipe combines all these flavors in one amazingly gluten-free treat.

Gluten-Free Salted Caramel-Pretzel Brownies

PREP TIME: 20 Minutes | START TO FINISH: 2 Hours 25 Minutes | *16 brownies*

1 box Betty Crocker Gluten Free brownie mix

¼ cup vegetable oil

3 tablespoons water

2 eggs

20 gluten-free caramels, unwrapped

½ cup gluten-free pretzel twists, coarsely crushed

½ teaspoon coarse sea salt

1 Heat oven to 350°F. Line 8- or 9-inch square pan with foil; spray foil with cooking spray (without flour).

2 Prepare brownies as directed on box for 8- or 9-inch square pan using oil, 2 tablespoons of the water and the eggs. Cool 1 hour.

3 In medium microwavable bowl, microwave caramels and remaining 1 tablespoon water uncovered on High 1 minute; stir. Microwave 30 to 45 seconds longer, stirring every 15 seconds, until melted and smooth. Spread over cooled brownies. Immediately sprinkle crushed pretzels over caramel; sprinkle with salt. Let stand about 30 minutes to set. Cut into 4 rows by 4 rows.

1 BROWNIE Calories 210; Total Fat 7g (Saturated Fat 3.5g, Trans Fat 0g); Cholesterol 30mg; Sodium 230mg; Total Carbohydrate 35g (Dietary Fiber 1g); Protein 2g **CARBOHYDRATE CHOICES:** 2

SCRATCH ORIGINAL SALTED CARAMEL–PRETZEL BROWNIES: Prepare and cool Frosted Fudge Brownies (page 182) as directed—except do not frost. Continue as directed in Step 3, using regular caramels and pretzels. (These brownies are not gluten free.)

Cooking Gluten Free? Always read labels to make sure *each* recipe ingredient is gluten free. Products and ingredient sources can change.

Betty's Kitchen Tips: Here's a little secret we know you'll love! Cutting brownies or any bar with a chewy and dense texture is much easier when you use a plastic knife.

How to Store: These gooey caramel-topped brownies taste great at room temperature, but to keep the caramel from getting too soft, store covered in the refrigerator.

RECIPE
#72

Festive Fruitcake Bars

PREP TIME: 20 Minutes | START TO FINISH: 1 Hour 55 Minutes | *24 bars*

BARS

- 1¼ cups all-purpose flour
- ¾ cup packed brown sugar
- ½ cup butter, softened
- 1 teaspoon grated orange zest
- ½ teaspoon baking soda
- ½ teaspoon ground cinnamon
- ¼ teaspoon salt
- 1 egg
- 2½ cups candied cherries
- 1 package (8 ounces) pitted dates, cut in half
- 1 cup coarsely chopped pecans or hazelnuts (filberts)

ORANGE GLAZE

- ⅓ cup granulated sugar
- 2 tablespoons orange juice

1 Heat oven to 350°F. Grease 13×9-inch pan with shortening; lightly flour.

2 In large bowl, mix 1 cup of the flour, the brown sugar, butter, orange zest, baking soda, cinnamon, salt and egg with spoon until well mixed. In medium bowl, mix remaining ¼ cup flour, the cherries, dates and pecans; stir into batter. Spread in pan.

3 Bake about 35 minutes or until toothpick inserted in center comes out clean. Cool completely in pan, about 1 hour.

4 In 1-quart saucepan, heat glaze ingredients over medium heat, stirring occasionally, until mixture thickens slightly. Drizzle cooled bars with glaze. Cut into 8 rows by 3 rows.

1 BAR Calories 190; Total Fat 7g (Saturated Fat 3g, Trans Fat 0g); Cholesterol 20mg; Sodium 85mg; Total Carbohydrate 29g (Dietary Fiber 2g); Protein 1g **CARBOHYDRATE CHOICES:** 2

Betty's Kitchen Tips: Line the baking pan with foil to make cleanup and cutting bars easy: Turn pan upside down and smooth foil over bottom and sides. Remove foil; turn pan right side up and ease foil into pan.

If you've never had homemade caramel corn, you're missing out. The rich, buttery caramel-coated popcorn and nuts are a treat for your mouth. It makes a wonderful hostess or holiday gift—if your family doesn't devour it first.

Caramel Corn

PREP TIME: 55 Minutes | **START TO FINISH:** 1 Hour 25 Minutes | *6 servings (1 cup each)*

6 cups popped popcorn	½ cup butter
½ cup toasted slivered almonds or walnut or pecan halves, if desired	2 tablespoons water
¾ cup firmly packed brown sugar	2 tablespoons light corn syrup
	⅛ teaspoon salt
	¼ teaspoon baking soda

1 Heat oven to 250°F. Spread popcorn in ungreased 15×10×1-inch baking pan. Sprinkle almonds over popcorn.

2 In large saucepan, mix brown sugar, butter, water, corn syrup and salt. Heat to boiling over medium heat. Boil 2 minutes, stirring constantly.

3 Remove saucepan from heat. Stir in baking soda until well mixed. Immediately pour mixture over popcorn and almonds; toss until coated.

4 Bake 15 minutes. Stir; bake 15 minutes longer. Stir; bake 5 minutes longer. Immediately scrape from pan and spread on foil or waxed paper. Cool 30 minutes before serving.

1 SERVING Calories 330; Total Fat 20g (Saturated Fat 10g, Trans Fat 0.5g); Cholesterol 40mg; Sodium 340mg; Total Carbohydrate 37g (Dietary Fiber 1g); Protein 1g **CARBOHYDRATE CHOICES:** 2½

POPCORN BALLS: Prepare as directed—except in Step 4, cool just until easy enough to handle. Dip your hands into cold water. Shape mixture into 2½-inch balls. Place on waxed paper; cool. Wrap individually or place in food-storage plastic bags and tie with twist tie, ribbon or raffia.

Betty's Kitchen Tips: Save prep time by using purchased popped popcorn.

Betty's Kitchen Tips: Use a large saucepan to prepare the caramel, as baking soda will cause mixture to foam up.

Betty's Kitchen Tips: To toast almonds, spread on cookie sheet; bake at 350°F for 5 to 7 minutes or until golden brown, stirring occasionally.

How to Store: Place in tightly covered container and store in a cool place up to 1 week.

Chocolate Caramels,
Chocolate-Topped
Sea Salt Caramels and
Caramels

> "This is the best recipe! For years, I used my mother's recipe, which was far too complicated. Not only is this simple, but every batch turns out perfectly. . . . These sell so well at church bazaars that there is a line of people waiting for them."—Betty lover

Caramels

PREP TIME: 40 Minutes | START TO FINISH: 2 Hours 40 Minutes | *64 or 81 candies*

2 cups sugar
2 cups whipping cream
¾ cup light corn syrup
½ cup butter, cut into pieces

1 Line 8- or 9-inch square pan with foil, leaving 1 inch of foil hanging over on two opposite sides of pan; grease foil with butter.

2 In 3-quart saucepan, heat all ingredients to boiling over medium heat, stirring constantly. Boil uncovered about 35 minutes, stirring frequently, to 245°F on candy thermometer or until small amount of mixture dropped into cup of very cold water forms a firm ball that holds its shape until pressed. Immediately spread in pan. Cool completely, about 2 hours.

3 Using foil, lift caramels out of pan; place on cutting board. Peel foil from caramels. Cut into 1-inch squares. Wrap individually in waxed paper or plastic wrap.

1 CANDY Calories 80; Total Fat 4g (Saturated Fat 2.5g, Trans Fat 0g); Cholesterol 10mg; Sodium 15mg; Total Carbohydrate 10g (Dietary Fiber 0g); Protein 0g **CARBOHYDRATE CHOICES:** ½

CHOCOLATE CARAMELS: Prepare as directed—except heat 2 oz unsweetened baking chocolate, chopped, with the sugar mixture.

CHOCOLATE-TOPPED SEA SALT CARAMELS: Prepare as directed—except after spreading caramel mixture into pan in Step 2, refrigerate about 1 hour or until completely cooled. In small microwavable bowl, microwave ½ cup semisweet chocolate chips and ½ teaspoon vegetable oil on High 30 to 45 seconds, stirring every 10 seconds, until chocolate is melted. Using spatula, spread chocolate evenly over caramel layer. Sprinkle with 1 teaspoon coarse sea salt or any coarse salt. Refrigerate about 30 minutes or until chocolate is set. Continue as directed in Step 3.

Betty's Kitchen Tips: Cut little rectangles of waxed paper ahead of time, so you're ready to wrap when it's time. Here's another secret: Cutting the caramels with a kitchen scissors is quicker and easier than using a knife.

How to Store: Caramels should be stored in a tightly covered container at room temperature.

This is almost the same recipe that was first printed in the 1950 version of the *Betty Crocker Picture Cookbook,* except we doubled the ingredients and added more corn syrup for a creamier fudge. That recipe instructed cooks to form the mixture into a roll and serve it as slices. We think little squares that you pop in your mouth are a lot easier to do—and eat!

Chocolate Fudge

PREP TIME: 35 Minutes | START TO FINISH: 2 Hours 35 Minutes | *64 candies*

4 cups sugar

1⅓ cups milk or half-and-half

¼ cup light corn syrup

¼ teaspoon salt

4 oz unsweetened baking chocolate, chopped

¼ cup butter, cut into pieces

2 teaspoons vanilla

1 cup chopped nuts, if desired

1 Grease bottom and sides of 8-inch square pan with butter.

2 In heavy 3-quart saucepan, cook sugar, milk, corn syrup, salt and chocolate over medium heat, stirring constantly, until chocolate is melted and sugar is dissolved. Cook, stirring occasionally, to 234°F on candy thermometer or until small amount of mixture dropped into cup of very cold water forms a soft ball that flattens when removed from water. Remove from heat. Stir in butter.

3 Cool mixture without stirring to 120°F, about 1 hour. (Bottom of saucepan will be lukewarm.) Add vanilla. Beat vigorously and continuously with wooden spoon 5 to 10 minutes or until mixture is thick and no longer glossy. (Mixture will hold its shape when dropped from a spoon.)

4 Quickly stir in nuts. Spread in pan. Let stand about 1 hour or until firm. Cut into 1-inch squares.

1 CANDY Calories 70; Total Fat 1.5g (Saturated Fat 1g, Trans Fat 0g); Cholesterol 0mg; Sodium 20mg; Total Carbohydrate 14g (Dietary Fiber 0g); Protein 0g **CARBOHYDRATE CHOICES:** 1

MOCHA NUT FUDGE: Prepare as directed—except add 4 teaspoons instant espresso powder or granules with the chocolate.

PEPPERMINT-TOPPED FUDGE: Prepare as directed—except after spreading fudge mixture in pan, immediately sprinkle with ¼ cup crushed peppermint candies; press lightly. Continue as directed.

CHERRY-CHOCOLATE FUDGE: Prepare as directed—except stir in ½ cup dried cherries with the nuts.

PENUCHE: Prepare as directed—except substitute 2 cups packed brown sugar for 2 cups of the granulated sugar and omit baking chocolate.

TOFFEE-CHOCOLATE FUDGE: Prepare as directed—except substitute 1 cup toffee bits for the nuts.

Betty's Kitchen Tips: To get an accurate reading, the thermometer should stand upright in the candy mixture, with the bulb or tip submerged in the candy mixture but not resting on the bottom of the pan. Read it at eye level. Watch the temperature closely—after 200°F, it goes up very quickly.

How to Store: Store fudge in a tightly covered container.

"I learned to cook using my Betty Crocker cookbook in the '90s. Still have that cookbook and I use it often." This evergreen recipe has shown up on many holiday cookie platters. We think it's an equally yummy treat for after-school snacks, hostess gifts or any time you're craving chocolate and peanut butter.

Chocolate-Covered Peanut Butter Candies

PREP TIME: 25 Minutes | START TO FINISH: 2 Hours 25 Minutes | *64 candies*

CANDIES
- ½ cup creamy peanut butter
- ¼ cup butter, softened
- ¼ cup chopped peanuts
- ½ teaspoon vanilla
- 2 cups powdered sugar
- 2 cups semisweet chocolate chips
- 1 tablespoon plus 1 teaspoon shortening

PEANUT BUTTER ICING
- ½ cup powdered sugar
- 2 tablespoons creamy peanut butter
- About 1 tablespoon milk

1 Line 8- or 9-inch square pan with foil, leaving 1 inch of foil overhanging at two opposite sides of pan. Grease foil with butter.

2 In medium bowl, mix ½ cup peanut butter, the butter, peanuts and vanilla. Stir in 2 cups powdered sugar, ½ cup at a time, until stiff dough forms. (Work in powdered sugar with hands if necessary.) If dough is crumbly, work in additional 1 tablespoon peanut butter. Pat mixture into pan. Cover; refrigerate about 1 hour or until firm. Remove from pan, using foil edges to lift. Cut into 8 rows by 8 rows.

3 Line cookie sheet with waxed paper or cooking parchment paper. In 1-quart saucepan, melt chocolate chips and shortening over low heat, stirring constantly. Remove from heat. Dip peanut butter squares, one at a time, into chocolate mixture. Place on waxed paper. Refrigerate uncovered about 30 minutes or until firm.

4 In small bowl, mix ½ cup powdered sugar and 2 tablespoons peanut butter. Beat in milk with whisk until smooth. Stir in additional milk, if necessary, 1 teaspoon at a time, until thin enough to drizzle.

5 Drizzle icing over tops of chocolate-covered squares. Refrigerate uncovered about 30 minutes or until firm.

1 CANDY Calories 80; Total Fat 4g (Saturated Fat 2g, Trans Fat 0g); Cholesterol 0mg; Sodium 20mg; Total Carbohydrate 9g (Dietary Fiber 0g); Protein 1g **CARBOHYDRATE CHOICES:** ½

Betty's Kitchen Tips: Use a dry fork to dip one candy at a time completely into melted chocolate. Lift up and draw fork across side of pan or bowl to remove excess chocolate. Using another fork, push candy off dipping fork onto cookie sheet.

How to Store: Store these delicious candies, loosely covered, in the refrigerator.

Unmatched Desserts

RECIPE #77

This type of cake got its name because originally one pound of each ingredient was used to make it. The citrusy-fresh hit of lemon, in both the cake and the glaze, makes this recipe a winner in our book.

Lemon Pound Cake

PREP TIME: 25 Minutes | START TO FINISH: 4 Hours | *10 servings*

CAKE

- 1⅓ cups granulated sugar
- ¾ cup butter, softened
- 2 tablespoons grated lemon zest
- 1 tablespoon fresh lemon juice
- 3 eggs
- 1½ cups all-purpose flour
- 1 teaspoon baking powder
- ¼ teaspoon salt
- ½ cup sour cream

GLAZE

- ½ cup powdered sugar
- 3 teaspoons fresh lemon juice

1 SERVING Calories 370; Total Fat 18g (Saturated Fat 10g, Trans Fat 0.5g); Cholesterol 100mg; Sodium 240mg; Total Carbohydrate 48g (Dietary Fiber 0g); Protein 4g **CARBOHYDRATE CHOICES:** 3

Make Ahead: The baked, cooled pound cake can be frozen to have on hand for when you want it. Wrap the unglazed cake in heavy-duty foil, then place in resealable food storage plastic bag. Freeze up to 2 to 3 months. Thaw at room temperature. Drizzle with glaze before serving.

How to Store: Cake will stay moist, stored in a tightly covered container at room temperature, up to 3 days.

1 Heat oven to 350°F. Grease 9×5-inch loaf pan with shortening; lightly flour.

2 In large bowl, beat granulated sugar and butter with electric mixer on medium speed until light and fluffy. Add 1 tablespoon lemon juice and the eggs; beat until well mixed. Beat in lemon zest and remaining cake ingredients on medium speed 1 to 2 minutes, scraping bowl occasionally, until well mixed. Pour evenly into pan.

3 Bake 1 hour to 1 hour 20 minutes or until toothpick inserted in center comes out clean. Cool in pan 15 minutes. Remove from pan onto cooling rack. Cool completely, about 2 hours.

4 In small bowl, mix powdered sugar and lemon juice, 1 teaspoon at a time, until thin enough to drizzle. Drizzle over top of cake.

"Cakes play an important role in the most significant moments in our lives."—Betty Crocker 1950. We love how our favorite chocolate cake is transformed with salted caramel buttercream. It's perfect for any occasion, from a simple picnic to an elaborate wedding.

Chocolate Cupcakes with Salted Caramel Buttercream

PREP TIME: 45 Minutes | START TO FINISH: 1 Hour 10 Minutes | *24 cupcakes*

CUPCAKES

- 2 cups all-purpose flour
- ⅔ cup unsweetened baking cocoa
- 1 teaspoon baking soda
- ½ teaspoon baking powder
- ¼ teaspoon salt
- ⅔ cup butter, softened
- 1⅓ cups granulated sugar
- 2 eggs
- 1½ teaspoons vanilla
- 1 cup buttermilk

FROSTING

- 1½ cups butter, softened
- 4 cups powdered sugar
- ½ cup salted caramel sauce
- 2 tablespoons milk
- 1 teaspoon vanilla

GARNISH

- 2 tablespoons salted caramel sauce, slightly warmed
- ½ teaspoon coarse sea salt

1 Heat oven to 350°F. Place paper baking cup in each of 24 regular-size muffin cups.

2 In medium bowl, mix flour, cocoa, baking soda, baking powder and ¼ teaspoon salt; set aside. In large bowl, beat ⅔ cup butter and the granulated sugar with electric mixer on medium speed, about 1 minute or until fluffy, scraping bowl occasionally. Beat in eggs, one at a time, until smooth. Stir in 1½ teaspoons vanilla. On low speed, gradually beat flour mixture into sugar mixture alternately with buttermilk, beating after each addition and scraping bowl occasionally, just until smooth. Spoon batter evenly into muffin cups, filling each about two-thirds full.

3 Bake 18 to 22 minutes or until toothpick inserted in center comes out clean. Cool in pan 10 minutes. Remove cupcakes from pan to cooling rack. Cool completely, about 30 minutes.

4 In large bowl, beat frosting ingredients with electric mixer on medium speed until smooth and spreadable. Frost cupcakes. Drizzle tops with caramel sauce; sprinkle with sea salt.

1 CUPCAKE Calories 339; Total Fat 17.5g (Saturated Fat 10.9g, Trans Fat 0.5g); Cholesterol 60.2mg; Sodium 183mg; Total Carbohydrate 45.8g (Dietary Fiber 1g); Protein 2.7g **CARBOHYDRATE CHOICES:** 3

Betty's Kitchen Tips: If you don't have enough pans to bake all the batter at once, cover and refrigerate remaining batter while baking the first batch. Cool pan completely before baking subsequent batches, adding 1 to 2 minutes to the bake time, if necessary.

Betty's Kitchen Tips: If you don't have a pastry bag to pipe on frosting, you can fill a large resealable plastic bag with frosting; seal bag. Cut off one small bottom corner; squeeze bag to pipe frosting on cupcakes.

Pumpkin-flavored foods get a lot of love, particularly in the fall. We love this recipe for so many reasons—its spice-flavored pumpkin cake, its rich cream cheese frosting . . . and for the fun of biting into the sugary, pecan-topped treats.

Spiced Pumpkin Cupcakes

PREP TIME: 40 Minutes | START TO FINISH: 1 Hour 50 Minutes | *24 cupcakes*

GARNISH
- ½ cup finely chopped pecans
- 3 tablespoons sugar

CUPCAKES
- 2⅓ cups all-purpose flour
- 2½ teaspoons baking powder
- 1½ teaspoons pumpkin pie spice
- ½ teaspoon salt

- 1 cup butter, softened
- 1¼ cups sugar
- 3 eggs
- 1 cup canned pumpkin (from 15-oz can; not pumpkin pie mix)
- 1 teaspoon vanilla
- ½ cup milk
- Double batch Cream Cheese Frosting (page 210)

1 Heat oven to 350°F. Place paper baking cup in each of 24 regular-size muffin cups. Or grease muffin cups with shortening or cooking spray; flour muffin cups.

2 In 8-inch nonstick skillet, cook pecans and 2 tablespoons of the sugar over low heat about 8 minutes, stirring frequently, until sugar is melted. Spoon and spread pecans onto sheet of waxed paper. Sprinkle with remaining 1 tablespoon sugar; toss to coat. Set aside.

3 In medium bowl, mix flour, baking powder, pumpkin pie spice and salt; set aside.

4 In large bowl, beat butter with electric mixer on medium speed 30 seconds. Gradually add 1¼ cups sugar, about one-fourth at a time, beating well after each addition and scraping bowl occasionally.

Beat 2 minutes longer. Add eggs one at a time, beating well after each addition. Beat in pumpkin and vanilla. On low speed, alternatively add flour mixture, about one-third at a time, beating just until blended. Spoon batter evenly into muffin cups, filling each about two-thirds full.

5 Bake 19 to 24 minutes or until golden brown and toothpick inserted in center comes out clean. Cool in pans 5 minutes; remove cupcakes from pans on cooling racks. Cool completely, about 30 minutes.

6 Frost cupcakes with frosting. Sprinkle top edge of frosted cupcakes with sugar-coated pecans; press lightly into frosting.

1 CUPCAKE Calories 330; Total Fat 15g (Saturated Fat 8g, Trans Fat 0g); Cholesterol 65mg; Sodium 230mg; Total Carbohydrate 43g (Dietary Fiber 1g); Protein 3g **CARBOHYDRATE CHOICES:** 3

EASY SPICED PUMPKIN CUPCAKES: Omit all cupcake ingredients—except 1½ teaspoons pumpkin pie spice and 1 cup canned pumpkin. Prepare 1 box yellow cake mix as directed on box—except use ½ cup water, ⅓ cup vegetable oil and 4 eggs, and add canned pumpkin and pumpkin pie spice. For frosting, use one 16-oz container cream cheese creamy ready-to-spread frosting. Frost and garnish as directed in recipe.

The original recipe for this lunch box favorite had you make your own applesauce first. We've skipped that step as well as tweaked the ingredients slightly—reducing the sugar, using pumpkin pie spice instead of several other spices—and topped it with a maple-nut buttercream, for an irresistible flavor that never goes out of style.

Applesauce Cake

PREP TIME: 15 Minutes | **START TO FINISH:** 2 Hours 15 Minutes | *12 servings*

CAKE

- 2½ cups all-purpose flour
- 1½ cups unsweetened applesauce
- 1¼ cups granulated sugar
- ½ cup butter, softened
- ½ cup water
- 1½ teaspoons baking soda
- 1½ teaspoons pumpkin pie spice
- 1 teaspoon salt
- ¾ teaspoon baking powder
- 2 eggs
- 1 cup raisins
- ⅔ cup chopped nuts

MAPLE-NUT BUTTERCREAM FROSTING

- 3 cups powdered sugar
- ⅓ cup butter, softened
- 1 to 2 tablespoons real maple or maple-flavored syrup
- ¼ cup chopped nuts

1 Heat oven to 350°F. Grease bottom and sides of 13×9-inch pan or two 8- or 9-inch round cake pans with shortening; lightly flour.

2 In large bowl, beat all cake ingredients except raisins and ⅔ cup nuts with electric mixer on low speed 30 seconds, scraping bowl constantly. Beat on high speed 3 minutes, scraping bowl occasionally. Stir in raisins and ⅔ cup chopped nuts. Pour into pan(s).

3 Bake rectangle 45 to 50 minutes or rounds 40 to 45 minutes or until toothpick inserted in center comes out clean. Cool rectangle completely in pan on wire rack. Cool rounds in pans 10 minutes; remove from pans to cooling rack. Cool completely, about 1 hour.

4 In large bowl, mix powdered sugar and butter with electric mixer on low until blended. Stir in 1 tablespoon of the maple syrup. Gradually beat in enough remaining maple syrup to make frosting smooth and spreadable. Frost rectangle or fill and frost round layers with frosting. Sprinkle cake with ¼ cup nuts.

1 SERVING Calories 550; Total Fat 20g (Saturated Fat 9g, Trans Fat 0.5g); Cholesterol 65mg; Sodium 400mg; Total Carbohydrate 86g (Dietary Fiber 2g); Protein 5g **CARBOHYDRATE CHOICES:** 6

BANANA CAKE: Prepare as directed—except substitute 1½ cups mashed ripe bananas (3 medium) for the applesauce and buttermilk for the water. Omit pumpkin pie spice and raisins. Increase baking powder to 1 teaspoon. Frost with Maple-Nut Buttercream Frosting (above) or Fudge Frosting (page 182).

Betty's Kitchen Tips: Puzzled by pumpkin pie spice? If you don't have it handy, then just combine ½ teaspoon ground cinnamon, ¼ teaspoon ground ginger, ⅛ teaspoon ground allspice and ⅛ teaspoon ground nutmeg to equal 1 teaspoon pumpkin pie spice.

"This is the best cake I ever had," writes a Betty fan. We couldn't agree more! It's hard to achieve a cake-like texture when you're baking gluten free. This recipe looks, tastes and eats like a traditional carrot cake. If you don't need to eat gluten free, you can make the classic variation.

Gluten-Free Carrot Cake

PREP TIME: 30 Minutes | **START TO FINISH:** 2 Hours 10 Minutes | *12 servings*

CAKE

- 1 cup Betty Crocker Gluten Free all-purpose rice flour blend
- 1 teaspoon ground cinnamon
- ½ teaspoon xanthan gum
- ½ teaspoon baking soda
- ½ teaspoon gluten-free baking powder
- ¼ teaspoon salt
- 1 cup granulated sugar
- 2 eggs
- ⅔ cup vegetable oil
- 1 teaspoon gluten-free vanilla
- 2 cups shredded carrots (about 2 medium carrots)
- ½ cup chopped pecans or walnuts

CREAM CHEESE FROSTING

- ⅓ cup butter, softened
- 6 oz gluten-free cream cheese (from 8-oz package), softened
- ¾ teaspoon gluten-free vanilla
- 2 cups powdered sugar
- 1 to 2 tablespoons milk
  Ground cinnamon, if desired

1 Heat oven to 350°F. Lightly grease bottom only of 8- or 9-inch round cake pan with shortening. Place cooking parchment paper round in bottom of pan; grease parchment paper.

2 In medium bowl, mix flour blend, cinnamon, xanthan gum, baking soda, baking powder and salt; set aside. In large bowl, beat granulated sugar and eggs with electric mixer on medium speed until light in color and fluffy. Add oil and 1 teaspoon vanilla; beat until smooth. On low speed, gradually beat in flour blend mixture just until blended. Stir in carrots and nuts. Pour batter into pan.

3 Bake 45 to 55 minutes or until toothpick inserted in center comes out clean. Cool in pan 15 minutes; remove from pan to cooling rack. Cool completely, about 30 minutes.

4 In medium bowl, beat butter, cream cheese and ¾ teaspoon vanilla with electric mixer on medium speed until creamy. On low speed, gradually beat in powdered sugar. Beat in milk, 1 teaspoon at a time, until desired spreading consistency. Place cake on serving plate; frost side and top with frosting. Sprinkle with cinnamon.

1 SERVING Calories 440; Total Fat 26g (Saturated Fat 8g, Trans Fat 0g); Cholesterol 60mg; Sodium 240mg; Total Carbohydrate 48g (Dietary Fiber 1g); Protein 3g **CARBOHYDRATE CHOICES:** 3

Continues

Gluten-Free Carrot Cake *continued*

CLASSIC CARROT CAKE: Prepare as directed—except grease bottom and side of cake pan with shortening; lightly flour (do not use cooking parchment paper). Omit cake ingredients. In Step 2, in large bowl beat ¾ cup sugar, ½ cup vegetable oil, 1 whole egg and 1 egg white with electric mixer on low speed 30 seconds. Add 1 cup all-purpose flour, 1 teaspoon ground cinnamon, ½ teaspoon baking soda, ¼ teaspoon salt and ½ teaspoon vanilla; beat on medium speed 1 minute. Stir in 1½ cups shredded carrots, ¼ cup drained crushed pineapple in juice, ½ cup chopped nuts and ¼ cup coconut. In Step 3, bake 30 to 35 minutes. Cool in pan 10 minutes before removing from pan to cooling rack. In Step 4, use original (not gluten-free) ingredients for the cream cheese frosting.

Cooking Gluten Free? Always read labels to make sure *each* recipe ingredient is gluten free. Products and ingredient sources can change.

Betty's Kitchen Tips: For easiest cutting, use a long, sharp knife and wipe clean between slices.

"WOW!! This was a great addition to my Memorial Day BBQ. I will be making this for the 4th of July, Labor Day and many other days to come." Mixing pudding mix with just a little milk before stirring in the whipped topping is the secret to making a frosting that isn't too runny.

Red, White and Blue Poke Cake

PREP TIME: 30 Minutes | START TO FINISH: 4 Hours 25 Minutes | *16 servings*

1 box Betty Crocker Super Moist™ white cake mix

1¼ cups water

⅓ cup vegetable oil

2 eggs

1 box (4-serving size) strawberry-flavored gelatin

1 cup boiling water

½ cup cold water

1 box (4-serving size) white chocolate–flavor instant pudding and pie filling mix

½ cup cold milk

1 container (8 oz) frozen whipped topping, thawed

1 cup sliced fresh strawberries

½ cup fresh blueberries

1 Heat oven to 350°F. Prepare cake mix as directed on box for 13×9-inch pan, using 1¼ cups water, the oil and eggs. Cool in pan on cooling rack 20 minutes.

2 With tines of fork, poke holes almost to bottom of warm cake about every ½ inch. In medium bowl, stir gelatin and boiling water until dissolved. Stir in cold water. Carefully pour mixture evenly over top of cake. Refrigerate, loosely covered, until serving time, at least 3 hours but no longer than 12 hours.

3 In large bowl, beat dry pudding mix and milk with whisk until blended and smooth (mixture will be thick). Gently stir in whipped topping. Drop by spoonfuls over top of cake; carefully spread until even. Arrange strawberries and blueberries on top of cake to look like flag.

1 SERVING Calories 250; Total Fat 9g (Saturated Fat 4g, Trans Fat 0g); Cholesterol 35mg; Sodium 240mg; Total Carbohydrate 39g (Dietary Fiber 1g); Protein 3g **CARBOHYDRATE CHOICES:** 2½

SCRATCH FESTIVE POKE CAKE: Instead of using the cake mix, substitute Silver White Cake (page 220) and prepare as directed through Step 3. In Step 4, bake as directed but cool in pan on cooling rack 20 minutes. Continue with Step 2 above.

Betty's Kitchen Tips: If you can't find white chocolate pudding mix, you can use vanilla instant pudding and pie filling mix.

Betty's Kitchen Tips: Be sure to poke the cake at least 50 to 60 times so there is plenty of gelatin in the cake! Wipe down the fork tines as you poke the cake. If tines aren't clean, they'll make "pokes" that are too large, which will mean you run out of gelatin before you've filled them all.

Betty's Kitchen Tips: The gelatin mixture needs time to set and cool completely in the poked cake, so for best results, refrigerate at least 3 hours before spreading pudding mixture on top.

Make Ahead: Prepare cake mix as directed on box for 13×9-inch pan. Cool in pan on cooling rack 20 minutes. Poke holes in warm cake with fork. Make gelatin mixture and carefully pour over top of cake. Loosely cover; refrigerate up to 12 hours. When ready to serve, make pudding mixture. Remove cake from refrigerator; uncover and top with pudding mixture. Decorate top with fruit.

How to Store: Store cake loosely covered in refrigerator.

Our food stylist Amy remembers this cake fondly from her childhood. She was so excited to make it but had forgotten how delicious it was. So we thought it was about time the recipe was dusted off and introduced to a new batch of cake lovers!

Oatmeal Cake with Broiled Topping

PREP TIME: 30 Minutes | START TO FINISH: 2 Hours 15 Minutes | *16 servings*

CAKE
- 1½ cups quick-cooking oats
- 1¼ cups boiling water
- 1 cup granulated sugar
- 1 cup packed brown sugar
- ½ cup butter, softened
- 1 teaspoon vanilla
- 3 eggs
- 1½ cups all-purpose flour
- 1 teaspoon baking soda
- ½ teaspoon baking powder
- ½ teaspoon salt
- 1½ teaspoons ground cinnamon
- ½ teaspoon ground nutmeg

TOPPING
- ⅔ cup packed brown sugar
- ¼ cup butter, melted
- 3 tablespoons half-and-half or milk
- 1 cup flaked coconut
- ½ cup chopped nuts

1 In small bowl, mix oats and boiling water; let stand 20 minutes. Meanwhile, heat oven to 350°F. Grease 13×9-inch pan with shortening or cooking spray; lightly flour.

2 In large bowl, beat granulated sugar, 1 cup brown sugar and ½ cup butter with electric mixer on medium speed until light and fluffy, scraping bowl occasionally. Beat in vanilla and eggs. Beat in oat mixture and remaining cake ingredients until well blended, scraping bowl occasionally. Spread batter evenly in pan.

3 Bake 35 to 45 minutes or until toothpick inserted in center comes out clean. Remove cake from oven.

4 Set oven control to broil. In small bowl, beat all topping ingredients except coconut and nuts with electric mixer on high speed until smooth. Stir in coconut and nuts. Spoon over hot cake; spread to cover.

5 Broil 4 to 6 inches from heat 1 to 2 minutes or until bubbly and light golden brown. Cool completely in pan on cooling rack, about 1 hour.

1 SERVING Calories 360; Total Fat 15g (Saturated Fat 8g, Trans Fat 0g); Cholesterol 60mg; Sodium 230mg; Total Carbohydrate 53g (Dietary Fiber 2g); Protein 4g **CARBOHYDRATE CHOICES:** 3½

Betty's Kitchen Tips: For a truly old-fashioned cake, use old-fashioned oats. You'll get a more oaty appearance, texture and flavor.

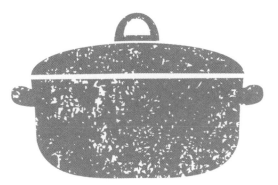

The rich depth of flavor that molasses brings to cake has been loved for generations. We have one word for this cake with sweet-tart cranberries and a rich butter sauce: yum!

Cranberry-Molasses Cake with Sweet Butter Sauce

PREP TIME: 20 Minutes | START TO FINISH: 1 Hour 25 Minutes | *20 servings*

CAKE

- 2 eggs
- ¾ cup sugar
- ¾ cup molasses
- ¾ cup water
- 2¼ cups all-purpose flour
- ¾ teaspoon salt
- ¾ teaspoon baking soda
- 2¼ cups fresh or frozen (thawed) cranberries

SWEET BUTTER SAUCE

- ¾ cup butter
- ¾ cup heavy whipping cream
- 1½ cups sugar

1 SERVING Calories 280; Total Fat 10g (Saturated Fat 6g, Trans Fat 0g); Cholesterol 45mg; Sodium 210mg; Total Carbohydrate 44g (Dietary Fiber 1g); Protein 2g **CARBOHYDRATE CHOICES:** 3

Betty's Kitchen Tips: If the sweet butter sauce has gotten too thick from cooling, heat over medium-low heat, stirring frequently, until warmed through. Or reheat in a glass measuring cup (50% power), just until warm.

How to Store: Store leftover cake and butter sauce covered, separately, in refrigerator. Let cake sit at room temperature at least 30 minutes before serving. Heat butter sauce in glass measuring cup uncovered on Medium (50%) 1 to 2 minutes, just until warm and pourable. Serve with cake.

1 Heat oven to 350°F. Grease bottom and sides of 13×9-inch pan with shortening or cooking spray.

2 In large bowl, beat eggs, ¾ cup sugar, the molasses and water with whisk. In medium bowl, mix flour, salt and baking soda. Stir flour mixture into liquid mixture just until moistened; fold in cranberries. Pour batter in pan.

3 Bake 37 to 42 minutes or until toothpick inserted in center comes out clean. Cool in pan on cooling rack 20 minutes.

4 In 2-quart saucepan, heat sauce ingredients over medium heat just to simmering, stirring constantly, until slightly thickened and sugar is dissolved. Remove from heat.

5 Spray edge of sharp knife with cooking spray; cut warm cake into 5 rows by 4 rows. Serve cake with warm sauce.

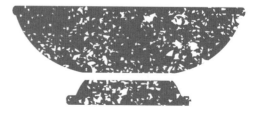

Appearing first in our 1950 "Big Red," this still remains our favorite white cake. If you've never had a scratch white cake, you will love the flavor this one has. With all the variations, you can make a different cake each time to suit your occasion.

Silver White Cake

PREP TIME: 20 Minutes | START TO FINISH: 2 Hours 15 Minutes | *12 servings*

CAKE

- 2¼ cups all-purpose flour or 2½ cups cake flour
- 1⅔ cups granulated sugar
- 3½ teaspoons baking powder
- 1 teaspoon salt
- ⅔ cup shortening
- 1¼ cups milk
- 1 teaspoon vanilla or almond extract
- ⅔ cup egg whites (about 5)

CREAMY VANILLA FROSTING

- 3 cups powdered sugar
- ⅓ cup butter, softened
- 1½ teaspoons vanilla
- 1 to 2 tablespoons milk

1 Heat oven to 350°F. Grease bottom and sides of 13×9-inch pan or 2 (9-inch) or 3 (8-inch) round cake pans with shortening; lightly flour.

2 In large bowl, beat all cake ingredients except egg whites with electric mixer on low speed 30 seconds, scraping bowl constantly, until smooth. Beat on high speed 2 minutes, scraping bowl occasionally. Beat in egg whites on high speed 2 minutes, scraping bowl occasionally. Pour into pan(s).

3 Bake 13×9-inch pan 40 to 45 minutes, 9-inch pans 30 to 35 minutes or 8-inch pans 23 to 28 minutes or until toothpick inserted in center comes out clean. Cool 13×9-inch cake in pan on cooling rack. Cool rounds in pans 10 minutes; remove from pans to cooling racks. Cool completely, about 1 hour.

4 In large bowl, mix powdered sugar and butter with electric mixer on low speed until blended. Stir in vanilla and 1 tablespoon of the milk. Gradually beat in just enough remaining milk to make frosting smooth and spreadable. If frosting is too thick, beat in more milk, a few drops at a time; if frosting is too thin, beat in small amount of powdered sugar.

5 Frost 13×9-inch cake or fill and frost round layers with frosting.

1 SERVING Calories 490; Total Fat 17g (Saturated Fat 6g, Trans Fat 0g); Cholesterol 15mg; Sodium 420mg; Total Carbohydrate 77g (Dietary Fiber 0g); Protein 5g **CARBOHYDRATE CHOICES:** 5

COOKIES 'N CREAM CAKE: Prepare as directed—except stir 1 cup crushed creme-filled chocolate sandwich cookies into batter after beating in egg whites. Garnish cake with additional crumbled creme-filled chocolate sandwich cookies.

MARBLE CAKE: Prepare as directed—except before pouring batter into pan(s), remove 1¾ cups of the batter; reserve. Pour remaining batter into pan(s). Stir 3 tablespoons unsweetened baking cocoa and ⅛ teaspoon baking soda into reserved batter. Drop chocolate batter by tablespoonfuls randomly onto white batter. Cut through batters with knife for marbled design. Bake and cool as directed in Step 3.

Betty's Kitchen Tips: If you prefer chocolate frosting, omit creamy vanilla frosting and prepare double batch (twice the amount of each ingredient) of Fudge Frosting (page 182).

Cookies 'n Cream
Cake

Chocolate cake with chocolate pudding, chocolate chips and chocolate glaze—no wonder this is a top-rated recipe on bettycrocker.com!

Chocolate Lover's Dream Cake

PREP TIME: 20 Minutes | START TO FINISH: 3 Hours 35 Minutes | *16 servings*

CAKE

- 1 box Betty Crocker Super Moist butter recipe chocolate cake mix
- ¾ cup chocolate milk
- ⅓ cup butter, melted
- 3 eggs
- 1 container (8 oz) sour cream
- 1 package (4-serving size) chocolate fudge instant pudding and pie filling mix
- 1 bag (12 oz) semisweet chocolate chips (2 cups)

GLAZE

- ¾ cup semisweet chocolate chips
- 3 tablespoons butter
- 3 tablespoons light corn syrup
- 1½ teaspoons water

1 SERVING Calories 400; Total Fat 20g (Saturated Fat 12g, Trans Fat 0g); Cholesterol 65mg; Sodium 390mg; Total Carbohydrate 50g (Dietary Fiber 2g); Protein 4g **CARBOHYDRATE CHOICES:** 3

Betty's Kitchen Tips: Measure the volume of your fluted tube cake pan using water to make sure it holds 12 cups. If pan is smaller than 12 cups, batter will overflow during baking.

Betty's Kitchen Tips: For milder chocolate flavor, you can use milk chocolate chips instead of semisweet.

How to Store: Store this decadent cake loosely covered at room temperature.

1 Heat oven to 350°F. Grease 12-cup fluted tube cake pan with shortening; lightly flour.

2 In large bowl, mix all cake ingredients except chocolate chips until well blended (batter will be very thick). Stir in chocolate chips. Spoon into pan.

3 Bake 56 to 64 minutes or until top springs back when touched lightly in center. Cool in pan 10 minutes. Turn pan upside down onto cooling rack or heatproof serving plate; remove pan. Cool completely, about 2 hours.

4 In 1-quart saucepan, heat glaze ingredients over low heat, stirring frequently, until chocolate chips are melted and glaze is smooth. Drizzle over cake.

This ever-popular cake, which dates back to the early 1900s, continues to be a top-ranked, frequently requested recipe from our Consumer Relations department as well as a fan favorite on bettycrocker.com.

Pineapple Upside-Down Cake

PREP TIME: 15 Minutes | START TO FINISH: 1 Hour 25 Minutes | *9 servings*

¼ cup butter

⅔ cup packed brown sugar

1 can (20 oz) pineapple slices or crushed pineapple in juice, drained

Maraschino cherries without stems, if desired

1⅓ cups all-purpose flour

1 cup granulated sugar

¾ cup milk

⅓ cup shortening

1½ teaspoons baking powder

½ teaspoon salt

1 egg

Sweetened Whipped Cream (right), if desired

1 SERVING Calories 390; Total Fat 14g (Saturated Fat 5g, Trans Fat 1.5g); Cholesterol 40mg; Sodium 270mg; Total Carbohydrate 63g (Dietary Fiber 1g); Protein 4g **CARBOHYDRATE CHOICES:** 4

SWEETENED WHIPPED CREAM: In chilled medium bowl, beat ½ cup heavy whipping cream, 1 tablespoon powdered sugar and ½ teaspoon vanilla with electric mixer on low speed until thickened. Gradually increase the speed to high until soft peaks form. Do not overbeat.

Betty's Kitchen Tips: We prefer the texture of this cake with shortening; however, if you wish, ¼ cup softened butter can be substituted for the shortening.

1 Heat oven to 350°F. In 9-inch square pan, melt butter in oven. Sprinkle brown sugar over butter. Arrange pineapple on top of brown sugar, cutting one or more slices into pieces if necessary to fit. Place cherry in center of each pineapple slice.

2 In large bowl, beat all remaining ingredients except Sweetened Whipped Cream with electric mixer on low speed 30 seconds, scraping bowl constantly. Beat on high speed 3 minutes, scraping bowl occasionally. Pour over pineapple.

3 Bake 50 to 55 minutes or until toothpick inserted in center comes out clean.

4 Immediately place heatproof plate upside down on pan; turn plate and pan over together. Let pan remain over cake a few minutes so brown sugar topping can drizzle over cake; remove pan. Serve warm with whipped cream.

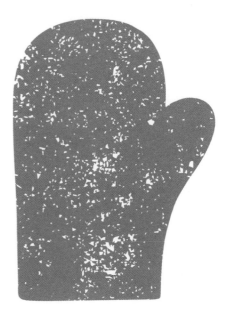

A family Christmas tradition for many, this showstopper is actually easy to make and as delicious as it looks. One bite, and you'll be thinking about it all year.

Bûche de Noël

PREP TIME: 40 Minutes | **START TO FINISH:** 1 Hour 25 Minutes | *10 servings*

CAKE
- 3 eggs
- 1 cup granulated sugar
- ⅓ cup water
- 1 teaspoon vanilla
- ¾ cup all-purpose flour
- 1 teaspoon baking powder
- ¼ teaspoon salt
  Powdered sugar

FILLING
- 1 cup whipping cream
- 2 tablespoons granulated sugar
- 1½ teaspoons instant coffee granules or crystals

CHOCOLATE BUTTERCREAM FROSTING
- ⅓ cup unsweetened baking cocoa
- ⅓ cup butter, softened
- 2 cups powdered sugar
- 1½ teaspoons vanilla
- 1 to 2 tablespoons hot water

1 Heat oven to 375°F. Line 15×10×1-inch pan with foil; grease foil with shortening or cooking spray.

2 In medium bowl, beat eggs with electric mixer on high speed about 5 minutes or until very thick and lemon colored. On low speed, gradually beat in 1 cup granulated sugar. Beat in water and 1 teaspoon vanilla. Gradually add flour, baking powder and salt, beating just until batter is smooth. Pour into pan, spreading to corners.

3 Bake 12 to 15 minutes or until toothpick inserted in center comes out clean. Immediately loosen cake from edges of pan; invert onto clean kitchen towel generously sprinkled with powdered sugar. Carefully remove foil. Trim off stiff edges of cake if necessary. While cake is hot, carefully roll cake and towel from narrow end. Cool on cooling rack at least 30 minutes.

4 In chilled medium bowl, beat filling ingredients with electric mixer on high speed until stiff peaks form. Unroll cake. Spread filling over cake. Roll up cake from long end, leaving towel on work surface. Place cake on serving platter.

5 In medium bowl, beat cocoa and butter with electric mixer on low speed until well blended. Beat in powdered sugar. Beat in vanilla and enough hot water, 1 teaspoon at a time, until frosting is smooth and spreadable.

6 For tree stump, cut off 2-inch diagonal slice from one end of cake. Attach stump to one long side using 1 tablespoon of the frosting. Frost cake and stump with remaining frosting. With tines of fork, make strokes in frosting to look like tree bark. Cover; refrigerate until ready to serve.

1 SERVING Calories 390; Total Fat 16g (Saturated Fat 9g, Trans Fat 0.5g); Cholesterol 100mg; Sodium 190mg; Total Carbohydrate 57g (Dietary Fiber 1g); Protein 4g **CARBOHYDRATE CHOICES:** 4

CHOCOLATE–ICE CREAM CAKE ROLL: Prepare cake as directed—except increase eggs to 4, and beat in ¼ cup unsweetened baking cocoa with flour. Substitute 1 to 1½ pints (2 to 3 cups) slightly softened ice cream for filling. Roll up cake as directed; wrap in plastic wrap and freeze while preparing chocolate buttercream frosting. Unwrap cake; frost with buttercream frosting. Loosely cover cake; freeze about 4 hours or until firm.

Continues

Bûche de Noël continued

ALMOND CREAM ROLL: Prepare cake as directed—except substitute ½ teaspoon almond extract for the vanilla. Prepare filling as directed—except substitute ¼ teaspoon almond extract for the coffee granules. Proceed with Step 5.

Betty's Kitchen Tips: You can omit cutting the roll to make the tree stump and simply frost the whole roll if you like. Traditionally served around the winter holidays, this is a cake you can serve year round!

Betty's Kitchen Tips: Decorate your yule log with beautiful sugared cranberries and rosemary sprigs: Thin light corn syrup with a little water. Dip fresh cranberries and fresh rosemary sprigs, one at a time, in mixture, rolling to coat completely; shake off excess. Roll in granulated sugar. Place on waxed paper until set. Arrange around log on serving platter, or on top of log. Chopped pistachios also make a nice garnish sprinkled over the frosting.

Make Ahead: You can make this cake up to 2 days in advance. Cover and refrigerate until ready to serve.

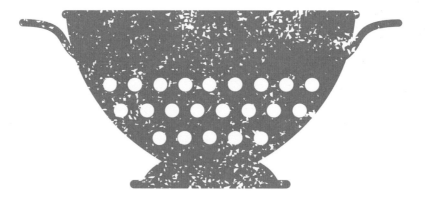

Angel food cake appeared in our very first *Betty Crocker's Picture Cookbook*. Over the years, we've updated the recipe, as the original was too sweet! We agonized over which version to include in this book—drizzled with glaze or topped with sweetened strawberries. We decided to give you both!

Angel Food Cake

PREP TIME: 20 Minutes | START TO FINISH: 3 Hours 25 Minutes | *12 servings*

CAKE

- 1½ cups egg whites (about 12)
- 1½ cups sugar
- 1 cup cake flour
- 1½ teaspoons cream of tartar
- 1½ teaspoons vanilla
- ½ teaspoon almond extract
- ¼ teaspoon salt

CHOCOLATE GLAZE

- ½ cup semisweet chocolate chips
- 2 tablespoons butter
- 2 tablespoons light corn syrup
- 1 to 2 teaspoons hot water

1 Let egg whites stand at room temperature for 30 minutes. Move oven rack to lowest position. Heat oven to 375°F.

2 In medium bowl, mix ¾ cup of the sugar and the flour; set aside. In large, clean, dry bowl, beat egg whites and cream of tartar with electric mixer on medium speed until foamy. Beat in remaining ¾ cup sugar, 2 tablespoons at a time, on high speed, adding vanilla, almond extract and salt with last addition of sugar. Continue beating until stiff and glossy. Do not underbeat.

3 Sprinkle flour mixture, ¼ cup at a time, over egg white mixture, folding in with rubber spatula just until flour mixture disappears. Spoon and spread batter into ungreased 10-inch angel food (tube) cake pan. Cut gently through batter with metal spatula or knife to break air pockets.

4 Bake 30 to 35 minutes or until cracks feel dry and top springs back when touched lightly. Immediately turn pan upside down onto heatproof bottle or funnel. Let hang about 2 hours or until cake is completely cool.

5 Loosen side of cake and along tube with knife or long metal spatula; remove from pan to serving plate, top-side up.

6 In 1-quart saucepan, heat all glaze ingredients except water over low heat, stirring frequently, until chocolate chips are melted. Cool about 10 minutes. Stir in hot water, 1 teaspoon at a time, until glaze is smooth and has consistency of thick syrup. Drizzle glaze over top of cake, allowing some of glaze to drip down side.

1 SERVING Calories 220; Total Fat 4g (Saturated Fat 2.5g, Trans Fat 0g); Cholesterol 5mg; Sodium 120mg; Total Carbohydrate 42g (Dietary Fiber 0g); Protein 4g **CARBOHYDRATE CHOICES:** 3

ANGEL FOOD CUPCAKES: Prepare as directed—except place paper baking cup in each of 24 regular-size muffin cups. Spoon ⅓ cup batter into each cup. Bake 17 to 23 minutes or until cracks in cupcakes feel dry and tops spring back when touched lightly. Cool in pans 10 minutes; remove from pans to cooling racks. Cool completely. Glaze if desired, or serve with whipped cream and fresh fruit.

Continues

Chocolate-Strawberry
Angel Food Cake

Angel Food Cake *continued*

CHOCOLATE CONFETTI ANGEL FOOD CAKE:
Prepare as directed—except stir 2 ounces semisweet
baking chocolate, grated, into sugar and flour in
Step 2.

STRAWBERRY-TOPPED ANGEL FOOD CAKE:
Prepare as directed—except omit glaze. In large
bowl, mix 6 cups sliced fresh strawberries and ¾ cup
sugar. Let stand while preparing the cake. Top cake
with some of the strawberries and their juice; serve
slices with remaining strawberries.

**CHOCOLATE-STRAWBERRY ANGEL FOOD
CAKE:** Prepare Strawberry-Topped Angel Food
Cake as directed—except drizzle chocolate glaze
over strawberries.

Betty's Kitchen Tips: We let the egg whites
stand at room temperature because warmer egg
whites will yield more volume when beaten than cold
egg whites.

RECIPE

#90

Two-Ingredient Pineapple Angel Food Cake

PREP TIME: 10 Minutes | START TO FINISH: 2 Hours 55 Minutes | *12 servings*

1 box Betty Crocker white angel food cake mix

1 can (20 oz) crushed pineapple in juice, undrained

1 Heat oven to 350°F.

2 In large bowl, beat dry angel food cake mix and crushed pineapple with electric mixer on low speed 30 seconds; beat on medium speed 1 minute. Pour into ungreased 10-inch angel food (tube) cake pan.

3 Bake 40 to 45 minutes or until top is dark golden brown and cracks feel very dry and not sticky. Do not underbake. Cool completely upside down as directed on cake mix box, about 2 hours. Run knife around edges; turn cooled cake out onto serving plate. Use serrated knife to cut into slices.

1 SERVING Calories 160; Total Fat 0g (Saturated Fat 0g, Trans Fat 0g); Cholesterol 0mg; Sodium 320mg; Total Carbohydrate 36g (Dietary Fiber 0g); Protein 3g **CARBOHYDRATE CHOICES:** 2½

How to Store: Store covered in refrigerator.

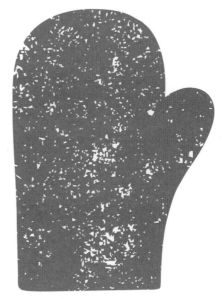

"The cake discovery of the century," chiffon cake was touted as "light as angel food, rich as butter cake." The recipe was given to Betty Crocker to "give the secret to the women of America." Betty refined and perfected the recipe so that anyone could make it with success.

Strawberry-Rhubarb Chiffon Cake

PREP TIME: 55 Minutes | START TO FINISH: 3 Hours 55 Minutes | *20 servings*

CAKE

- 1¾ cups all-purpose flour
- 2 teaspoons baking powder
- 1 teaspoon salt
- 1¼ cups granulated sugar
- ½ cup vegetable oil
- 6 eggs, separated
- 10 strawberries, pureed in blender or food processor (about ¾ cup)
- 22 drops red food color
- ½ teaspoon cream of tartar

FILLING AND GLAZE

- 1 cup chopped fresh rhubarb or frozen (thawed and drained) cut rhubarb
- 2 teaspoons grated lemon zest
- ¼ cup granulated sugar
- 1 tablespoon water
- 1½ cups quartered fresh strawberries
- 1 cup whipping cream
- 1½ cups powdered sugar

1 Heat oven to 350°F.

2 In large bowl, mix flour, baking powder, salt and ½ cup of the granulated sugar until blended. Add oil, egg yolks, pureed strawberries and food color; beat with electric mixer on medium speed about 2 minutes or until blended. Set aside.

3 Wash and dry beaters. In medium bowl, beat egg whites and cream of tartar with electric mixer on medium speed about 1 minute 30 seconds or until soft peaks form. Gradually add remaining ¾ cup granulated sugar, beating until stiff peaks form. Fold one-third of the egg white mixture into the batter gently but thoroughly. Fold in remaining egg white mixture until no white streaks remain.

Pour into ungreased 10-inch angel food (tube) cake pan. Tap pan on counter to remove air bubbles.

4 Bake 50 to 60 minutes or until toothpick inserted in center of cake comes out clean. Immediately turn pan upside down onto heatproof bottle or funnel. Let hang about 2 hours or until cake is completely cool.

5 Meanwhile, in 1-quart saucepan, heat rhubarb, lemon zest, ¼ cup granulated sugar and the water to boiling over medium heat. Reduce heat to medium-low; simmer until soft and thoroughly cooked, about 3 minutes. Remove from heat; set aside to cool, about 30 minutes. Stir in quartered strawberries.

6 In medium bowl, beat ½ cup of the whipping cream and 1 tablespoon of the powdered sugar until stiff peaks form. Fold in ½ cup of the cooled strawberry-rhubarb mixture. Reserve remaining mixture for top of cake.

7 Run knife around edges and tube; turn cooled cake out onto serving plate. Cut 1-inch layer off top of cake; set aside. Cut tunnel into cake 1 inch deep and 1 inch wide; discard tunnel scraps. Fill tunnel with strawberry-rhubarb cream mixture. Replace top of cake.

8 To make glaze, in medium bowl, stir together remaining ½ cup whipping cream and remaining powdered sugar (almost 1½ cups) until smooth. Spoon glaze over top of cake, letting it run down

Continues

Strawberry-Rhubarb Chiffon Cake *continued*

side. Top with reserved strawberry-rhubarb mixture just before serving.

1 SERVING Calories 270; Total Fat 12g (Saturated Fat 4g, Trans Fat 0g); Cholesterol 70mg; Sodium 190mg; Total Carbohydrate 38g (Dietary Fiber 1g); Protein 3g **CARBOHYDRATE CHOICES:** 2½

Betty's Kitchen Tips: To prepare fresh rhubarb, trim the ends and discard all traces of the leaves (rhubarb leaves are poisonous). Scrub the stalks and cut into pieces about 1 inch in length.

How to Store: Store covered in refrigerator.

Betty on Social Media

Sharing and networking with Betty fans meant something a little different in years gone by. In addition to her widely popular radio program, Betty shared recipes, cooking and baking tips and other home management advice in the form of several newsletters and a Betty Crocker magazine. Included with the food-related content were articles ranging from how to pick a Christmas tree, to the latest research on feeding babies solid foods and advice on reviewing your homeowner's insurance policy.

Today, Betty's social media is widely comprehensive. New cookbooks and e-books come out of the Betty Crocker Kitchens each year (nearly 400 to date), including the *Betty Crocker Cookbook* (affectionately known as "Big Red"), which has sold more than 75 million copies in 12 editions. From Facebook and Instagram to bettycrocker.com (one of the most popular cooking websites, with more than 14 million visits per month) to Betty Crocker on Alexa, answering cooking and baking questions, Betty Crocker has evolved to serve consumers' changing lifestyles. Always trending with the times to continue to be a trusted resource in the kitchen, she never really ages!

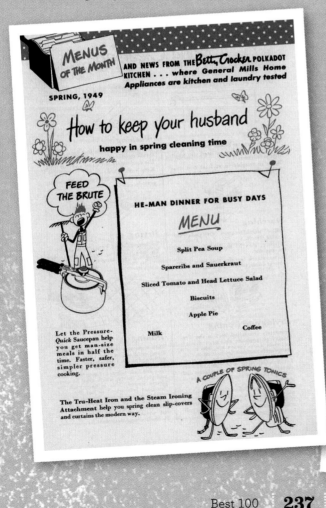

If you want an easy apple pie recipe, this is it! Impossibly Easy pies from Bisquick have been popular since their debut in the 1970s. Sweet or savory, they always turn out delicious.

Impossibly Easy French Apple Pie

PREP TIME: 25 Minutes | START TO FINISH: 1 Hour 15 Minutes | *6 servings*

FILLING

- 3 cups sliced peeled apples (3 medium)
- 1 teaspoon ground cinnamon
- ¼ teaspoon ground nutmeg
- ½ cup Original Bisquick mix
- ½ cup granulated sugar
- ½ cup milk
- 1 tablespoon butter, softened
- 2 eggs

STREUSEL

- ½ cup Original Bisquick mix
- ¼ cup chopped nuts
- ¼ cup packed brown sugar
- 2 tablespoons cold butter

    Ice cream, if desired

1 SERVING Calories 330; Total Fat 13g (Saturated Fat 5g, Trans Fat 0g); Cholesterol 80mg; Sodium 270mg; Total Carbohydrate 49g (Dietary Fiber 2g); Protein 5g **CARBOHYDRATE CHOICES:** 3

IMPOSSIBLY EASY FRENCH PEAR PIE: Prepare as directed—except substitute 3 cups sliced peeled pears for apples.

Betty's Kitchen Tips: Some of our favorite varieties of apples for baked pies and desserts are Granny Smith, Braeburn and Rome. If you like, use a few varieties together.

How to Store: Cover any remaining pie and store in refrigerator.

1 Heat oven to 325°F. Grease 9-inch glass pie plate with shortening or cooking spray.

2 In medium bowl, mix apples, cinnamon and nutmeg; place in pie plate. In same bowl, stir remaining filling ingredients until well blended. Pour over apple mixture in pie plate.

3 In small bowl, mix streusel ingredients with fork until crumbly; sprinkle over filling.

4 Bake 40 to 45 minutes or until knife inserted in center comes out clean. Let stand 5 minutes before serving. Serve warm or cool with ice cream.

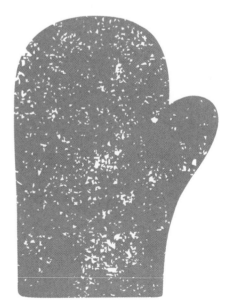

> "This is an old recipe from 30 years ago. I made this when first married, forgot about it or lost the recipe. So easy to make. Can't mess this pie up . . . love it. Thank you for bringing it back."

Impossibly Easy Coconut Pie

PREP TIME: 10 Minutes | **START TO FINISH:** 1 Hour 5 Minutes | *8 servings*

½ cup Original Bisquick mix

1 cup flaked or shredded coconut

¾ cup sugar

¼ cup butter, softened

1½ teaspoons vanilla

2 cups milk

4 eggs

Sweetened Whipped Cream (page 225) or frozen whipped topping, thawed, if desired

1 SERVING Calories 260; Total Fat 12g (Saturated Fat 8g, Trans Fat 0g); Cholesterol 20mg; Sodium 220mg; Total Carbohydrate 32g (Dietary Fiber 0g); Protein 4g **CARBOHYDRATE CHOICES:** 2

1 Heat oven to 350°F. Grease 9-inch pie plate with shortening or cooking spray.

2 In medium bowl, mix all ingredients until blended. Pour into pie plate.

3 Bake 50 to 55 minutes or until golden brown and knife inserted in the center comes out clean. Cool pie on cooling rack completely before serving. Serve with Sweetened Whipped Cream.

Betty's Kitchen Tips: Read coconut packages closely and you'll notice that there are two types available: flaked and shredded. Flaked coconut is cut into small pieces and is drier than shredded coconut. Either type works well in most recipes, but using shredded results in a more moist and chewy finished product.

How to Store: Cover any remaining pie and store in refrigerator.

If you want a pie that people remember, this is it. What makes a great pie is a flaky crust that plays the supporting role to the perfectly baked apples and spices. Let your fork be the judge.

Classic Apple Pie

PREP TIME: 30 Minutes | START TO FINISH: 3 Hours 20 Minutes | *8 servings*

TWO-CRUST PASTRY

- 2 cups plus 2 tablespoons all-purpose flour
- 1 teaspoon salt
- ⅔ cup cold shortening
- 3 to 5 tablespoons ice-cold water

PIE FILLING

- ½ cup sugar
- ¼ cup all-purpose flour
- ¾ teaspoon ground cinnamon
- ¼ teaspoon ground nutmeg
- Dash salt
- 6 cups thinly sliced peeled tart apples (6 medium)
- 2 tablespoons cold butter, if desired

TOPPING

- 2 teaspoons water
- 1 tablespoon sugar

1 Heat oven to 425°F.

2 In medium bowl, mix 2 cups plus 2 tablespoons flour and salt. Cut in shortening, using pastry blender or fork, until mixture forms coarse crumbs the size of small peas. Sprinkle with water, 1 tablespoon at a time, and toss with fork until all flour is moistened and pastry almost leaves side of bowl (1 to 2 teaspoons more water can be added if necessary).

3 Gather pastry into ball; divide pastry in half and shape into two rounds on lightly floured surface.

4 Using floured rolling pin, roll one pastry round on lightly floured surface into a circle 2 inches larger in diameter than upside-down 9-inch glass pie plate. Fold pastry circle in quarters and place in pie plate. Unfold and ease into plate, being careful not to stretch pastry, which can cause it to shrink when baked.

5 In large bowl, mix all pie filling ingredients except apples and butter. Stir in apples. Spoon into pastry-lined pie plate. Cut butter into small pieces; sprinkle over apples. Cover with top pastry; cut slits in pastry. Gently fold edge of top and bottom pastry under to seal together, pressing lightly to edge of pie plate. Press tines of fork dipped into flour into pastry edge to secure to pie plate. Or flute edge as desired.

6 Brush top crust with 2 teaspoons water; sprinkle with 1 tablespoon sugar. Cover edge with 2- to 3-inch-wide strip of foil to prevent excessive browning.

7 Bake 40 to 50 minutes (remove foil during last 15 minutes of baking) or until crust is golden brown and juice begins to bubble through slits in crust. Cool on cooling rack at least 2 hours.

1 SERVING Calories 420; Total Fat 21g (Saturated Fat 7g, Trans Fat 2g); Cholesterol 10mg; Sodium 330mg; Total Carbohydrate 53g (Dietary Fiber 3g); Protein 4g **CARBOHYDRATE CHOICES:** 3½

CLASSIC PEACH PIE: Prepare as directed—except use ⅔ cup sugar and ⅓ cup flour in filling. Decrease cinnamon to ¼ teaspoon and omit nutmeg. Substitute sliced peeled fresh peaches (6 to 8) for apples. Stir in 1 teaspoon lemon juice with peaches. Decrease butter to 1 tablespoon.

BLUEBERRY PIE: Prepare as directed—except use 1¼ cups sugar; substitute ½ cup cornstarch for flour in filling. Decrease cinnamon to ½ teaspoon and

Continues

Classic Apple Pie *continued*

omit nutmeg and salt. Substitute fresh blueberries for apples. Stir in 1 tablespoon lemon juice with blueberries. Decrease butter to 1 tablespoon. Bake pie 35 to 45 minutes.

STRAWBERRY-RHUBARB PIE: Prepare as directed—except use 2 cups sugar; increase flour in filling to ½ cup. Omit cinnamon, nutmeg and salt. Add 1 teaspoon grated orange zest with flour, if desired. Substitute 3 cups cut (½-inch pieces) rhubarb and 3 cups sliced fresh strawberries for apples. Decrease butter to 1 tablespoon. Bake pie 50 to 55 minutes.

CHERRY PIE: Prepare as directed—except use 1⅓ cups sugar; increase flour in filling to ½ cup. Omit cinnamon, nutmeg and salt. Substitute pitted fresh sour cherries for apples. Bake pie 35 to 45 minutes.

Betty's Kitchen Tips: Cut apples thinly and evenly to ensure they cook all the way through.

Make Ahead: This pie can be prepared ahead and frozen unbaked or baked. If unbaked, don't cut slits in top pastry. Freeze loosely covered, with room around it so that the pasty edge won't get broken or misshapen during freezing. Once frozen, wrap tightly. (At this point, other items can touch up against the pie.) Wrap baked and cooled pie tightly and freeze. To thaw and bake unbaked pie: Unwrap and cut slits in top crust. Bake at 425°F for 15 minutes. Reduce oven to 375°F, bake 30 to 45 minutes longer or until juices begin to bubble through slits. To thaw baked pie: Unwrap at room temperature or to serve warm, unwrap and thaw at room temperature 1 hour, then bake in 375°F oven 35 to 40 minutes or until warm.

RECIPE #95

Peanut Butter Ice Cream Pie

PREP TIME: 25 Minutes | **START TO FINISH:** 6 Hours 30 Minutes | *8 servings*

CHOCOLATE COOKIE CRUMB CRUST

- 1½ cups finely crushed thin chocolate wafer cookies (24 cookies)
- ¼ cup butter, melted

CHOCOLATE–PEANUT BUTTER SAUCE

- 1 cup bittersweet or semisweet chocolate chips (6 oz)
- ¼ cup creamy peanut butter
  Dash salt
- ¼ cup whipping cream
- 1 tablespoon light corn syrup

FILLING

- 2 pints (4 cups) peanut butter ice cream
- 1 pint (2 cups) chocolate or vanilla ice cream
- ½ cup salted cocktail peanuts

GARNISH

- 1 cup chocolate-covered peanuts, coarsely chopped

1 Heat oven to 350°F.

2 In medium bowl, mix crust ingredients. Press mixture firmly and evenly against bottom and side of 9-inch glass pie plate. Bake 10 minutes. Cool on cooling rack 15 minutes. Place in freezer while preparing filling.

3 Meanwhile, place both ice creams in refrigerator to soften, about 20 to 30 minutes.

4 In medium bowl, stir together chocolate chips, peanut butter and salt. In 1-quart saucepan, heat whipping cream and corn syrup over low heat until hot but not boiling. Pour over peanut butter mixture; cover bowl with plastic wrap. Let stand 1 minute; uncover and stir until smooth.

5 Spread ⅓ cup of the chocolate–peanut butter sauce in bottom of chilled crust. Sprinkle with cocktail peanuts. Spoon 3 cups of the peanut butter ice cream over top; spread evenly. Quickly and carefully spread with ½ cup of the sauce over ice cream (it will start to freeze). With small ice cream scoop or tablespoon, alternate scoops of chocolate ice cream and remaining 1 cup peanut butter ice cream over top, covering pie and achieving bubble look.

6 Sprinkle chocolate-covered peanuts over top. Drizzle with remaining chocolate–peanut butter sauce. Cover with plastic wrap and freeze 5 hours or until firm. Place pie in refrigerator 30 minutes to soften slightly before cutting.

1 SERVING Calories 720; Total Fat 43g (Saturated Fat 21g, Trans Fat 1g); Cholesterol 70mg; Sodium 380mg; Total Carbohydrate 69g (Dietary Fiber 5g); Protein 13g **CARBOHYDRATE CHOICES:** 4½

Betty's Kitchen Tips: There are several peanut butter-flavored varieties of ice cream available. Use your favorite, or try different flavors each time you make this pie.

Betty's Kitchen Tips: If the chocolate-peanut butter sauce begins to harden while you're assembling the pie, microwave it uncovered in a microwavable bowl on High in 10-second increments until softened.

We love this recipe because the taste and texture remind us of a traditional Key lime pie. You won't feel like you have to "settle." A bite of this sweet-tangy pie will win you over, too.

Gluten-Free Key Lime Pie

PREP TIME: 20 Minutes | START TO FINISH: 3 Hours 45 Minutes | *8 servings*

CRUST
- 9 gluten-free graham crackers (from 7.5-oz box), finely crushed (1½ cups)
- 6 tablespoons butter, melted
- 3 tablespoons sugar

FILLING
- ¾ cup bottled or fresh Key lime juice
- 2 cans (12 oz each) sweetened condensed milk (not evaporated)
- 4 egg yolks
- 1 or 2 drops green food color, if desired
- 1½ cups Sweetened Whipped Cream (page 225)

  Key lime slices, if desired

1 SERVING Calories 670; Total Fat 27g (Saturated Fat 17g, Trans Fat 1g); Cholesterol 160mg; Sodium 490mg; Total Carbohydrate 95g (Dietary Fiber 0g); Protein 10g **CARBOHYDRATE CHOICES:** 6

Cooking Gluten Free? Always read labels to make sure *each* recipe ingredient is gluten free. Products and ingredient sources can change.

Betty's Kitchen Tips: Key limes, grown in Florida, are smaller and rounder than the more familiar green (Persian) limes, and their color is more yellow than green. Although Key limes are less widely available than Persian limes, bottled Key lime juice is generally available. Either lime works well in this recipe.

How to Store: Cover and store leftover pie in the refrigerator.

1 Heat oven to 350°F.

2 In medium bowl, stir crust ingredients until well mixed. Reserve 2 tablespoons crust mixture for garnishing top of pie before serving. Press remaining mixture firmly and evenly against bottom and side of 9-inch glass pie plate.

3 In medium bowl, beat filling ingredients with electric mixer on medium speed about 1 minute or until well blended. Pour into crust.

4 Bake 18 to 22 minutes or until center is set. Cool in pie plate on cooling rack 15 minutes. Cover; refrigerate until chilled, at least 3 hours but no longer than 3 days.

5 When ready to top, spread with Sweetened Whipped Cream and Key lime slices; garnish with remaining crumb mixture.

Always popular, dump cakes are more like a crisp than a cake. Originally, recipes used a cake mix, "dumping" just a few ingredients into the pan, for an extra-easy dessert. We love this version made with just a few scratch ingredients instead of cake mix, giving it rich homemade flavor and juicy texture.

Buttery Peach Dump Cake

PREP TIME: 15 Minutes | START TO FINISH: 1 Hour | *8 servings*

6 cups fresh or frozen sliced peeled peaches, thawed

⅓ cup sugar

1⅓ cups all-purpose flour

¾ cup sugar

⅔ cup old-fashioned or quick-cooking rolled oats

1¼ teaspoons baking powder

¼ teaspoon salt

¾ cup butter, melted

Vanilla ice cream or whipped cream, if desired

1 SERVING Calories 420; Total Fat 18g (Saturated Fat 11g, Trans Fat 0.5g); Cholesterol 45mg; Sodium 290mg; Total Carbohydrate 60g (Dietary Fiber 5g); Protein 4g **CARBOHYDRATE CHOICES:** 4

Betty's Kitchen Tips: Substitute 2 cups fresh or frozen mixed berries (do not thaw) for 2 cups of peaches. Increase bake time to 40 to 45 minutes.

1 Heat oven to 350°F. Spray bottom and sides of 13×9-inch pan with cooking spray. Place peaches in pan. Sprinkle with ⅓ cup sugar; mix gently. Spread evenly in pan.

2 In medium bowl, mix remaining ingredients except butter and ice cream; sprinkle evenly over peaches. Drizzle with melted butter, tilting pan to cover as much of cake mix as possible.

3 Bake 38 to 42 minutes or until light golden brown and bubbly around the edges. Cool 15 minutes before serving. Serve warm with ice cream.

RECIPE

#98

Chocolate Cookie–Brownie Lush

PREP TIME: 35 Minutes | **START TO FINISH:** 6 Hours | *24 servings*

BROWNIE BASE
- 1 box (18.3 oz) Betty Crocker fudge brownie mix
- ½ cup vegetable oil
- 3 tablespoons water
- 3 eggs

LAYERS
- 1 package (8 oz) cream cheese, softened
- 1 cup powdered sugar
- 1 container (12 oz) frozen whipped topping, thawed
- 1½ cups finely crushed creme-filled chocolate sandwich cookies (about 16 cookies)
- 2 boxes (4-serving size each) chocolate instant pudding and pie filling mix
- 3 cups cold milk

TOPPING
- ½ cup coarsely crushed creme-filled chocolate sandwich cookies (about 4 cookies)

1 Heat oven to 350°F. Spray bottom only of 13×9-inch pan with cooking spray.

2 In medium bowl, mix dry brownie mix, oil, water and eggs until well blended. Spread in pan.

3 Bake 22 to 25 minutes or until toothpick inserted 2 inches from side comes out almost clean. Cool completely, about 1 hour.

4 In large bowl, beat cream cheese and powdered sugar with electric mixer on medium speed until smooth, scraping bowl frequently. Beat in 2 cups of the whipped topping. Spread over brownie. Sprinkle 1½ cups finely crushed cookies over cream cheese mixture.

5 In medium bowl, beat dry pudding mix and milk with whisk about 2 minutes or until thick.

Spread over cookie layer. Drop remaining whipped topping by spoonfuls over pudding layer; spread evenly. Cover; refrigerate 4 hours.

6 When ready to serve, sprinkle with topping. Cut into 6 rows by 4 rows.

1 SERVING Calories 310; Total Fat 13g (Saturated Fat 6g, Trans Fat 0g); Cholesterol 35mg; Sodium 300mg; Total Carbohydrate 44g (Dietary Fiber 1g); Protein 3g **CARBOHYDRATE CHOICES:** 3

SCRATCH CHOCOLATE COOKIE–BROWNIE LUSH: Prepare as directed—except in Step 2, prepare a double batch (using twice the amount of each ingredient) of Brownies from Frosted Fudge Brownies (page 182), and bake in 13×9-inch pan. You might need to increase bake time a few minutes.

Betty's Kitchen Tips: To quickly soften cream cheese, remove from wrapper and place on microwavable plate. Microwave uncovered on Medium (50%) 1 minute to 1 minute 30 seconds or just until softened.

Betty's Kitchen Tips: Finely crush the cookies so the layer will hold together by using a food processor or placing them in a resealable freezer plastic bag and using a rolling pin or meat mallet.

Make Ahead: Prepare as directed—except do not top dessert with crushed cookies. Cover and refrigerate up to 24 hours. Sprinkle with cookies just before serving.

How to Store: Cover and refrigerate any remaining pieces in pan.

A recipe for apple dumplings was available free in Gold Medal flour bags, as noted in a 1938 advertisement, and has been included in many of the company's cookbooks over the years, beginning with the 1904 Christmas edition of the *Gold Medal Flour Cook Book*.

Apple Dumplings

PREP TIME: 55 Minutes | START TO FINISH: 1 Hour 35 Minutes | *6 servings*

Two-Crust Pastry (page 243)

6 small cooking apples (Golden Delicious, Braeburn or Rome; about 3 inches in diameter)

3 tablespoons raisins, dried cranberries or dried cherries, if desired

3 tablespoons chopped nuts, if desired

2½ cups packed brown sugar

1⅓ cups water

2 tablespoons butter, softened

¼ teaspoon ground cinnamon

Half-and-half or whipping cream or Sweetened Whipped Cream (page 225), if desired

1 Heat oven to 425°F. Make pastry as directed—except roll two-thirds of the pastry into 14-inch square; cut into 4 (7-inch) squares. Roll remaining pastry into 14×7-inch rectangle; cut into 2 (7-inch) squares.

2 Peel and core apples; place 1 apple on each pastry square. In small bowl, mix raisins and nuts; fill apples with mixture. Moisten corners of pastry squares. Bring two opposite corners up over apple and pinch together. Repeat with remaining corners; pinch edges of pastry to seal.

3 Place dumplings in ungreased 13×9-inch (3-quart) glass baking dish. In 2-quart saucepan, heat brown sugar, water, butter and cinnamon to boiling over high heat, stirring frequently. Carefully pour syrup around dumplings.

4 Bake about 40 minutes, spooning syrup over dumplings two or three times, until crust is golden and apples are tender when pierced with small knife or toothpick. Serve warm or cooled, with cream.

1 SERVING Calories 840; Total Fat 27g (Saturated Fat 8g, Trans Fat 0g); Cholesterol 10mg; Sodium 450mg; Total Carbohydrate 144g (Dietary Fiber 3g); Protein 5g **CARBOHYDRATE CHOICES:** 9½

Betty's Kitchen Tips: You'll need to stick to 3-inch apples. If you use larger apples, the dough squares will not be large enough to seal.

RECIPE

#100

Easy Peach Cobbler

PREP TIME: 10 Minutes | **START TO FINISH:** 1 Hour 20 Minutes | *6 servings*

- 1 cup sugar
- 3 cups sliced peeled peaches (about 4 medium) or 1 can (29 oz) sliced peaches, drained
- 1 tablespoon cornstarch

- 1 cup Original Bisquick mix
- 1 cup milk
- ½ teaspoon ground nutmeg
- ½ cup butter, melted
  Sweetened Whipped Cream (page 225), if desired

1 SERVING Calories 410; Total Fat 18g (Saturated Fat 11g, Trans Fat 0.5g); Cholesterol 45mg; Sodium 330mg; Total Carbohydrate 58g (Dietary Fiber 1g); Protein 3g **CARBOHYDRATE CHOICES:** 4

Betty's Kitchen Tips: Add sparkle and texture to top of cobbler by sprinkling decorator sugar crystals over dough before baking.

Betty's Kitchen Tips: Serve warm cobbler with ice cream, a drizzle of caramel topping and a sprinkle of toasted pecans for an over-the-top, tummy-warming treat.

Betty's Kitchen Tips: Need to serve more? You can make a double batch (using twice the amount of each ingredient) and use a 13×9-inch (3-quart) glass baking dish. You might need to add a few minutes to the bake time.

1 Heat oven to 375°F.

2 In medium bowl, stir sugar, peaches and cornstarch until peaches are evenly coated with sugar mixture. Spoon into ungreased 8-inch square (2-quart) glass baking dish.

3 In another medium bowl, stir Bisquick mix, milk and nutmeg with whisk or fork until mixed; stir in butter until blended. Spoon over peaches.

4 Bake 50 to 60 minutes or until golden brown. Let stand 10 minutes before serving. Serve warm with Sweetened Whipped Cream.

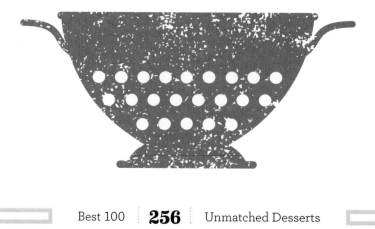

Metric Conversion Guide

VOLUME

U.S. UNITS		CANADIAN METRIC		AUSTRALIAN METRIC	
¼	teaspoon	1	mL	1	ml
½	teaspoon	2	mL	2	ml
1	teaspoon	5	mL	5	ml
1	tablespoon	15	mL	20	ml
¼	cup	50	mL	60	ml
⅓	cup	75	mL	80	ml
½	cup	125	mL	125	ml
⅔	cup	150	mL	170	ml
¾	cup	175	mL	190	ml
1	cup	250	mL	250	ml
1	quart	1	liter	1	liter
1½	quarts	1.5	liters	1.5	liters
2	quarts	2	liters	2	liters
2½	quarts	2.5	liters	2.5	liters
3	quarts	3	liters	3	liters
4	quarts	4	liters	4	liters

WEIGHT

U.S. UNITS	CANADIAN METRIC		AUSTRALIAN METRIC	
1 ounce	30	grams	30	grams
2 ounces	55	grams	60	grams
3 ounces	85	grams	90	grams
4 ounces (¼ pound)	115	grams	125	grams
8 ounces (½ pound)	225	grams	225	grams
16 ounces (1 pound)	455	grams	500	grams
1 pound	455	grams	0.5	kilogram

NOTE: The recipes in this cookbook have not been developed or tested using metric measures. When converting recipes to metric, some variations in quality may be noted.

MEASUREMENTS

INCHES	CENTIMETERS
1	2.5
2	5.0
3	7.5
4	10.0
5	12.5
6	15.0
7	17.5
8	20.5
9	23.0
10	25.5
11	28.0
12	30.5
13	33.0

TEMPERATURES

FAHRENHEIT	CELSIUS
32°	0°
212°	100°
250°	120°
275°	140°
300°	150°
325°	160°
350°	180°
375°	190°
400°	200°
425°	220°
450°	230°
475°	240°
500°	260°

Recipe Testing and Calculating Nutrition Information

RECIPE TESTING:

- Large eggs and 2% milk were used unless otherwise indicated.

- Fat-free, low-fat, low-sodium or lite products were not used unless indicated.

- No nonstick cookware and bakeware were used unless otherwise indicated. No dark-colored, black or insulated bakeware was used.

- When a pan is specified, a metal pan was used; a baking dish or pie plate means ovenproof glass was used.

- An electric hand mixer was used for mixing only when mixer speeds are specified.

CALCULATING NUTRITION:

- The first ingredient was used wherever a choice is given, such as ⅓ cup sour cream or plain yogurt.

- The first amount was used wherever a range is given, such as 3- to 3½-pound whole chicken.

- The first serving number was used wherever a range is given, such as 4 to 6 servings.

- "If desired" ingredients were not included.

- Only the amount of a marinade or frying oil that is absorbed was included.

Index

Note: Page references in *italics* indicate photographs.

P

Hungry for more?

Don't miss these other great Betty Crocker cookbooks

Betty Crocker
SNACKS
Easy Ways to Satisfy Your Cravings

Betty Crocker
Cookies
Irresistibly Easy Recipes for Any Occasion

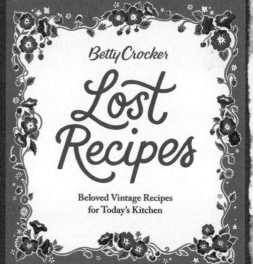

Betty Crocker
Lost Recipes
Beloved Vintage Recipes for Today's Kitchen

Betty Crocker
Make It in One
Dinner in One Pan, One Pot, One Sheet Pan...and More

Betty Crocker
Learn with Betty
ESSENTIAL RECIPES AND TECHNIQUES TO BECOME A CONFIDENT COOK

Betty Crocker
Cookbook
Everything you need to know to cook from scratch